Yes to Mission

DOUGLAS WEBSTER

SCM PRESS LTD
BLOOMSBURY STREET LONDON

To

MAX WARREN

with admiration, affection
and gratitude for inspiration, friendship
and encouragement

FIRST PUBLISHED 1966
© SCM PRESS LTD 1966
PRINTED IN GREAT BRITAIN BY
BILLING AND SONS LTD
GUILDFORD AND LONDON

CONTENTS

PREFACE

THIS is a book about the Christian Mission. There is a growing recognition that the subject is important. There is also quite extraordinary confusion and sentimentalism about it. The following pages are an attempt to clear away some of the confusion and all of the sentimentalism.

The debt I owe to the thinking of others is immense and most of all to him to whom this little book is dedicated, without whose constant insistence I should never have written anything. But much of the material has been drawn from conversations and observations in many parts of the world during my own missionary journeys. To have been allowed to make these is the greatest privilege of my life. A good deal of what is written here has been given in some form or other in lectures to clergy schools and theological colleges, but it has been largely re-shaped.

In a book of a strictly prescribed size limits have to be imposed. I have therefore selected what I consider to be the four main aspects of mission that need stressing today. Chapter 1 is concerned with various contemporary attitudes and misconceptions. Chapter 2 is frankly theological, but mission without theology is like a runaway truck. Chapter 3 is about the Churches in Asia and Africa and some of their problems. Chapter 4 seeks to explore the relation of mission to the Cross of Jesus Christ and in the light of this to portray something of the cross of the modern missionary. Mission today is rightly thought of as the Church's task in all six continents, and there are thousands of Christians who are as deeply committed to this work in their own country as are those who leave their homeland and serve overseas. It has not been possible to draw out the implications of the themes of these chapters for everyone everywhere. The perceptive reader will no doubt do this for himself. To concentrate on the western missionary is not to ignore the rest. Their changing situation and contribution need understanding and appraisal.

I have to thank Canon Max Warren and Dr Norman Goodall for great kindness in reading through the typescript and making most valuable suggestions and corrections.

To the best of my knowledge and intention all biblical quotations come from the Revised Standard Version in the case of the Old Testament and from the New English Bible in the case of the New—unless otherwise stated.

D. W.

I

MISUNDERSTANDING OF MISSION
Towards a Reassessment

A Buddhist monk was addressing a meeting of the Student Christian Movement in Oxford. In his talk, almost as an aside, he said:

> To the eastern religious it looks as if Christianity has reached the stage in adolescence when the child is slightly ashamed of his father and embarrassed when talking about him.

An English lady, who had always been an ardent supporter of missions in her parish church, paid a visit to East Africa. Such was the shock produced by what she saw that she said:

> I have been wasting my time all these years, knitting clothes for people who have no need of them, giving money for a Church which has plenty of rich members, with better houses and better cars than we have, who only put a penny in the collection on Sunday. Not another gift for missions, not another working party!

A young man, who had gone as a missionary to Africa to teach on the staff of an important boys' school, wrote in a letter:

> In practice I find that I am not expected to do more than fill the role that is assured to me. I am welcomed as one of a team of teachers turning out boys with school certificates and Christian principles. I do not think I am welcomed as one who might want to take initiative in evangelism, for example, either inside or outside the school. To suggest a change in religion or education

on the local or the wider scale is an implied criticism of what exists, and we all know that criticism is the one thing that is 'out' in Africa.

At a dinner party somewhere in Malaysia there is a mixed group of Europeans and Indians. One of the guests, a young Indian clergyman, not in the least intimidated by the presence of his bishop or his host and hostess, all Europeans, bursts out:

The reason why missionaries come here is to escape their duties in their own country. It is much easier to convert people out here than it is in England.

A distinguished Indian scholar and diplomat has written:

It will hardly be denied that, in spite of the immense and sustained effort made by the Churches with the support of the lay public of the European countries and America, the attempt to conquer Asia for Christ has definitely failed.[1]

A leading German missionary statesman, addressing the Ghana Assembly of the International Missionary Council in 1958, was comparing the situation with that of thirty years earlier when a previous Assembly was held in Jerusalem in 1928:

Then missions had problems, but they were not a problem themselves. There was no question that the initiative in witness and action was with western missions as they stood. Today we do not speak of the initiative of western missions but only of their contribution. But more than this: we are uncertain about their patterns as they are, and even more, the historic, basic conceptions of missions are being questioned.[2]

*   *   *

[1] K. M. Panikkar, *Asia and Western Dominance*, George Allen and Unwin 1953, 454.
[2] W. Freytag in *The Ghana Assembly of the I.M.C.* (edited by R. K. Orchard), Edinburgh House Press 1958, 138.

THESE six extracts will serve to introduce the theme of this chapter and indeed of the whole book. To some of the problems we shall keep returning in subsequent chapters, looking at them from various angles. We have begun by bringing them together so that they may set the scene. It is not untroubled. The quotations, however, indicate four factors which can be described either as areas of misunderstanding or things which create misunderstanding about mission. We may call them: the mood of uncertainty, the disposal of myths, the dilemma of the missionary, the measurement of failure and success.

THE MOOD OF UNCERTAINTY

The first and the last of the quotations underline this, the one by a Buddhist, the other by a Christian. The Buddhist sees Christians as being somewhat ashamed and embarrassed by their religion, reluctant to speak about God. The Christian admits the bewilderment which faces the missionary enterprise today. Both look at Christianity from quite different points of view, but both sense much the same thing. If we try to discover or analyse the causes of our embarrassment on the one hand and our bewilderment on the other, we find that there are a number of elements to be sorted out.

In the first place there is a marked distinction between eastern and western attitudes to religion. In the East religion is as common and easy a topic for conversation as the weather is in England. The devout and the slack alike are willing to discourse on religion for hours. On journeys in India I have myself found the greatest readiness, even eagerness, for such discussion in trains, buses, aircraft. Few conversations proceed for long without turning this way. In the West there is a natural reticence to introduce religion into general talk. This is partly because of the desire to avoid controversial subjects —and religion has been highly controversial since the sixteenth century—and partly because of an awareness of our own relative ignorance about something sacred and important. Even some most deeply Christian people would often feel as great a sense of indelicacy in talking about their religion as in discussing the intimacies of their married life and love. The reasons for this need not detain us beyond noting that whereas in the East religion is strongly communal, in the West it is largely private, a matter of individual choice and personal faith; and in the East religion still pervades the larger part of life and culture, but in the West, now considerably secularized, religion is to a great extent separated and independent from life and culture. In the East a religious attitude is almost inevitable; in the West it is entirely optional.

Nevertheless, when ample allowance has been made for different attitudes to religion as between East and West, the Buddhist's remark was a shrewd and penetrating insight into our mood. Just because it is a word of understanding, it is also a word of judgment. Which of us has never been in the least ashamed or embarrassed because of our Christian faith? St Paul's splendid declaration, 'I am not ashamed of the Gospel' (Rom. 1.16), suggests that perhaps some of the earliest Christians were ashamed of it, and that even he had passed through a period when he felt that way too. In II Timothy 1.11, 12 there is a reiteration of this 'I am not ashamed', and Timothy himself is exhorted: 'Do not be ashamed then of testifying to our Lord' (II Tim. 1.8 RSV). From the very beginning there has been that in the Christian message which can conjure up a sense of shame. Had not Jesus himself warned his followers about this in a context where he is speaking about the inherent contradictions of the Gospel? 'If anyone is ashamed of me and mine (or, my words) in this wicked and godless age, the Son of Man will be ashamed of him, when he comes in the glory of his Father and of the holy angels' (Mark 8.38). The New Testament as a whole witnesses to the fact that the source and centre of this 'being ashamed' was the cross, the historic Cross on which the Messiah was crucified, and the principle of the cross which is basic to the Christian way of life. This had always been a scandal, a stumbling-block, a hindrance. It kept the Jews from belief, because they could not contemplate a *crucified* Messiah; it kept the Greeks from belief, because they could not discern the wisdom they looked for in such a spectacle. Yet, on the other side of faith, 'to those who have heard his call, Jews and Greeks alike, he is the power of God and the wisdom of God' (I Cor. 1.24). 'He' is the Christ nailed to the cross. The heart of St Paul's argument is that Christianity is not self-evident. That is the *embarrassing* thing about it. We cannot prove it. We cannot reason people into it. We cannot say that it represents the world's highest wisdom, for it is the very opposite to the world's wisdom, even at its best, as Paul contended so forcibly in I Corinthians 1 and 2. Nobody can arrive at it unaided, nor by their own goodness, nor by their own thinking. No one can attain salvation by his own effort. On this Christianity stands or falls. At this point Christianity is in stark contrast to all oriental religion. For oriental religion can claim to be self-evident; it does have its own inner logic; it does, in the last analysis, insist that man must save himself. And whereas the self-denial, the bearing of the cross, which Christianity inculcates, is the *result* of the experience of salvation through Christ, in oriental religion it is the *means* of salvation.

This absence of self-evidence in the Christian position, coupled with its insistence on God experiencing a brutal death at the hands of men, makes it unpalatable to 'the natural man' (I Cor. 2.14 AV and RV). It inhibits the Christian from casual conversation about his faith, simply because it does not fit into the ordinary religious categories in a comfortable way. It cannot easily be discussed, not only because its final aim is to elicit a decision from every man, but also because the Spirit of God alone can enable any man to understand it. So Paul argues: 'we are interpreting spiritual truths to those who have the Spirit. . . . A man who is unspiritual refuses what belongs to the Spirit of God; it is folly to him; he cannot grasp it, because it needs to be judged in the light of the Spirit' (I Cor. 2.13, 14).

If these considerations explain to some extent the feeling of embarrassment and shame which overtakes the typical western Christian in religious matters, especially in speaking about them, they do not altogether excuse it. It is true that there always has been an element of scandal about the Gospel, and that this is also associated with the unique claims Christians make for Jesus Christ; but it is also true that in spite of all this, from the beginning there have been those who were willing to witness to their Lord and to their faith without reticence or hesitation. The Buddhist monk was detecting a degree of reticence which would have been quite foreign to the early Church and to the great creative and expansive periods of Christian history. To him western Christianity looked tired and shy and unsure of itself. This is a phenomenon which we must take seriously. The missionary Christianity which invaded Africa and the East in recent centuries was none of these things. It had a confidence and buoyancy comparable to that of the apostolic age of the Church, when, notwithstanding the 'offence of the Gospel', there was a compulsiveness about bearing witness to it. The essence of the Gospel was as uncongenial to the culture of the Graeco-Roman world of the first century as it is to the scientific-technological world of the twentieth. It was every whit as contradictory to commonly held and popular assumptions. Yet we find the first Christians clinging tenaciously to the most offensive aspect of the Gospel —'There is no salvation in anyone else at all, for there is no other name under heaven granted to men, by which we may receive salvation' (Acts 4.12)—and at the same time they continue in the face of all threats to preach. When the authorities order them to refrain, their reply is simple and direct : 'Is it right in God's eyes for us to obey you rather than God? Judge for yourselves. We cannot possibly give up speaking of things we have seen and heard' (Acts 4.19, 20). They were not compulsive talkers; they were compulsive witnesses. The compulsion was the pressure of the Holy Spirit. Because the Spirit himself bears witness to Jesus—this is part of his work—those who are filled with the Spirit will do likewise (see John 15.26, 27). 'I cannot help myself : it would be misery to me not to preach,' wrote Paul (I Cor. 9.16). 'The lion has roared; who will not fear? The Lord God has spoken; *who can but prophesy?*' (Amos 3.8).

Except in the Roman Catholic Church (and even there rumblings are to be heard!) and among conservative evangelical groups and fundamentalist sects, this sense of missionary compulsion is today largely lacking. But it was not to these that the Buddhist monk was speaking or referring. There seems to be some discernible relation between the urge to mission and the certainty about doctrine. Moreover, although there are those who assume that the less dogma the Church holds the easier its missionary enterprise will become, this does not seem to be the case in practice. On the contrary, the more vague Christians allow themselves to be about the basic truths of the faith, the more indifferent they appear to grow about their obligation in respect of mission; whereas the authoritarian Christian groups, whose doctrines are set out with clarity and proclaimed with conviction, are those which seem to be the most effective in mission. Nevertheless, it must also be recognized that most forms of fundamentalist mission are presupposing a world which no longer exists and providing answers to questions that men are no longer asking. It has yet to be seen whether their present effectiveness will carry over from one generation to the next and provide both continuity and solidarity.

Our concern here, however, is with our own mood of uncertainty. This is exemplified in a series of books which appeared in close succession: *Soundings* (ed. A. R. Vidler) in 1962, *Honest to God* (by J. A. T. Robinson), *The Secular Meaning of the Gospel* (by Paul van Buren) and *Objections to Christian Belief* (ed. A. R. Vidler), all in 1963. In 1964 Bishop James Pike of San Francisco published *A Time for Christian Candour*. These writers share a common radicalism. They are anxious to re-state the faith in terms intelligible to that elusive creature, 'modern man'. They are all Anglicans, most of them theologians. Their thinking has been inspired by Rudolf Bultmann, Dietrich Bonhoeffer and Paul Tillich, three of this century's theological giants. To discuss the contents of these works would be to digress from our main theme. Reactions to them have varied. Some have welcomed them as making Christianity more intellectually relevant, if not respectable. Others have felt that in leaning over backwards to make the Gospel easy for the intellectual, they reduce it to something unrecognizable. Opinions will vary. But on any showing all these writers

are wanting a less dogmatic Christianity. Intellectually at least
and in varying degrees they have felt something of the shame
and embarrassment sensed by the Buddhist observer, and this
is reflected in the attitudes of many of the younger generation
of Christians, particularly those who are not conservatives or
traditionalists.

It may be readily admitted that there is much to be ashamed
about in the churches and in some of our outward expressions
of Christianity. We have all fallen short; there is none
righteous, no, not one. Again we may admit that not many
people will now wish to equate the Christian faith with any
one confessional formulation of it, such as the Tridentine
Decrees, the Augsburg Confession, the Westminster Confession, or the Thirty-Nine Articles. But when full allowance
has been made for the historic and sociological conditioning
of such confessions, and the process of lopping off or laying
quietly aside has been fully indulged in, one question remains :
Where does this stop? Is there behind all the accretions of
Christian history and controversy an essential, unalterable
Gospel, transcending all denominational formulas? Is there a
hard core concerning which we may say with Paul 'I am not
ashamed'? Is there a bed-rock on which we can take our stand
and say with Luther : Here I stand, I can no other?

I believe there is. For there is a basis in history for the whole
Christian faith, even though the faith which enables us to be
Christians is itself a gift from God (Eph. 2.8) and not primarily
a deduction from history. That basis may be found in St
Paul's great statement in four monosyllables : 'God was in
Christ' (II Cor. 5.19), and in its corollary : 'Jesus is Lord' (I Cor.
12.3). The truth in these assertions has been challenged, of
course, by non-Christian thinkers. It has not been challenged
or denied by the most radical Christian theologians. The
Christian may question everything else; he can hardly question
this and still remain Christian in the sphere of thought and
faith. Nevertheless, if these statements are true, as Christians
believe and understand them to be, we have here a sufficient
basis and reason for mission. If God was in Christ, if Jesus is
Lord, this is something that everybody ought to know.

Let us acknowledge that the Church must move out of some of its entrenched positions, as it has constantly had to do in the past. Let us acknowledge the difficulties that some find in definitions of the Trinity and the Incarnation phrased in Greek philosophical terms, the problems of miracles, the inspiration of Scripture, and all the rest. Every generation of theologians must wrestle with these and they are important. But while it is no longer possible to be dogmatic about so many of these doctrines in the way our fathers were, let us avoid the other extreme of assuming that there is nothing of which we may be reasonably sure and that Christians can no longer make any positive statements. If any Church reaches this position it has no future. For the essence of the Gospel is that it is able to make certain statements about Jesus Christ with complete assurance. From this point of view the Gospel *is* dogmatic and cannot be anything else if it is to remain Gospel. It is as dogmatic as any news-item which may affect us, for good or ill, any day. Unless the Church and its theologians can return soon to a much more positive and ringing declaration of the eternal Gospel, we shall not be in a position to play a very significant part in the next—and probably unusually difficult —phase of the Christian mission.

Such a statement as 'God was in Christ' or its equivalents 'The Word became flesh' (John 1.14) or 'God sent forth his Son' (Gal. 4.4) do in themselves provide an adequate basis for mission, because they constitute news of a kind so dynamic as to affect every human being for all time. But the Gospel necessarily expands them. 'God was in Christ reconciling the world to himself, not counting their trespasses against them.' 'The Word became flesh and dwelt among us, full of grace and truth,' which follows an earlier statement, 'To all who received him, who believed in his name, he gave power to become children of God' (John 1.12 RSV). 'God sent forth his Son, born of woman, born under the law, to redeem those who were under the law, so that we might receive adoption as sons.' At the very least, then, the apostolic understanding of the Gospel is of a deed of God in history affecting the life and destiny of every man in time and in eternity. Whether we go all the way with 'the new theologians' or not, *none of this is in dispute*. But the terminology and presentation, which are in dispute, have been allowed to obscure the heart of it all and to turn away attention from the one supreme name and event and invitation which the Church is constituted and commissioned to announce and proclaim. Behind all the problems, all the documents, all the creeds and liturgies, there stands one figure, Jesus Christ. By virtue of his incarnation and his crucifixion he allows himself to be assailed, questioned, doubted, discussed. But he does not disappear when the discussion ends or the speakers weary. He remains—the same for ever. The Gospel is about him. Of him no Christian has cause to be ashamed—or embarrassed.

If the Christian mission is to be discharged, locally, nationally, universally, there must be a recovery of what, for want of a better expression, we may perhaps call a limited dogma. 'In the accepted Christian meaning the term (dogma) signifies a religious truth established by Divine Revelation and defined by the Church.'[1] We need not apply this too rigidly, but we must recognize that unless the Christian Church has something definite to say about Jesus Christ—and this, surely, must involve dogma—it is hardly qualified to speak about anything else. After all, mission implies that the Church does have something to say. But what?

It is not usually difficult for Christians to agree on the basic elements of the Gospel itself. Nor are these 'fundamentals' seriously affected by modern theology, though the way of stating them has changed. If the Church is to have a Gospel to be missionary about, and if that Gospel is to bear any relation to what we find in the New Testament, then it ought to contain four irreducible elements.

First, there is the person and character of Jesus Christ. He really did live. He was remarkably different from all other men, though himself undoubtedly man. He made an astonishing and unforgettable impact upon his contemporaries, and

[1] *Oxford Dictionary of the Christian Church*, ed. F. L. Cross: art. on Dogma.

this impact has continued through all subsequent history and shows no signs of diminishing.

Second, there is the teaching of Jesus Christ. He said certain things about God, about life, about the Kingdom of God, and about human destiny. No one had spoken with the same authority about these matters before, nor has anyone since.

Third, there is the death of Jesus Christ. That it was brought about by the wickedness and false choices of men, few will deny. That it achieved some kind of permanent moral victory, making possible a new relationship between God and men, based on forgiveness and acceptance, issuing in reconciliation and peace, has been the conviction of Christians from the beginning. The death of Jesus was a turning-point in history. God was active in it, achieving his perfect will through sacrifice of an unique quality.

Fourth, death did not put an end to Jesus in the way it has put an end to all other men. The first Christians believed that he had put an end to death: he had conquered it. They were convinced that he had risen from the dead, that his mission was accomplished, that his presence was to be with them always, and that by his resurrection a new era had begun, there was a New Being which in Christ and through Christ all men could enter.

Many Christians would want to add a great deal more than this to the Gospel—that is another matter. What is being urged here is that we cannot have less, if we are to retain the Gospel at all. But if these four basic truths of the Gospel are really accepted and believed, they constitute a sufficient basis and they provide a sufficient message for the Christian mission. There is little reason to suppose that anything of validity in the new theology is seriously threatening these beliefs. Such doctrines as the Virgin Birth, Hell, the Return of Christ to earth, do raise difficulties which are felt more by some people than by others. But the Gospel does not stand or fall with these, neither does the Christian mission.

Is it not time, therefore, to distinguish between the many things about which we can never have certainty and those basic themes of the Gospel which Christians *know by faith* to be true? At the edges of faith there is much that baffles, but the missionary concern is not with the periphery but with the centre. In a letter written a week before he died, the great Bishop Lightfoot of Durham wrote: 'I find that my faith suffers nothing by leaving a thousand questions open, so long as I am convinced on two or three main lines.'[1] That was in 1889!

We may be grateful for the new modesty of some theologians. We must admit readily that there are very few things of which we may have objective certainty. But we must realize also that there are certain things concerning which Christians can say, both with humility and conviction, 'we know'. If Christian faith and experience have any continuity we may use these words as an expression of conviction and assurance in the same manner as they are repeatedly used in the First Epistle of St John (e.g. 2.21; 3.5; 3.14; 5.13, 15, 18, 19, 20). A mood of uncertainty about the heart of the Gospel, the Lord of the Church, and the Saviour of the world, is unworthy of Christians and bodes ill for the future of missions if it is allowed or encouraged to persist. Describing the first mission to Thessalonica St Paul wrote: 'When we brought you the Gospel, we brought it not in mere words but in the power of the Holy Spirit, *and with strong conviction*, as you know well' (I Thess. 1.5). Christian, even theological, humility is not synonymous with vagueness.

THE DISPOSAL OF MYTHS

If any subject needs demythologizing, that subject is mission. The myths whch surround it are not to be found in the Scriptures but in people's minds. 'Missionary work' is associated with raising money, doing good, and a particular kind of preaching. Many of those who actively support missions are unaware of their successes or failures. A measure of success is to be seen in the growth of the Church in almost every country in the world. (There is as yet no indigenous church in Saudi Arabia, Afghanistan, Tibet or Outer Mongolia.) A measure of

[1] Quoted by A. R. Vidler, *Christian Belief*, SCM Press 1950, 116.

failure is to be seen in the slenderness of the missionary effort in many countries once the foreign missionary is withdrawn or his initiative is restricted. We shall be returning to this problem later. But despite all the effort that has gone into missionary education, at least in the European churches, there are many who still believe what they want to believe. It is therefore a peculiarly painful and disillusioning business when they discover for themselves that they were wrong.

The English lady visiting East Africa is a case in point. A sight of the real thing produced a traumatic experience. It need not have done, had she not clung to the myths and failed to reach a proper perspective. As a tourist she doubtless saw what Africans wanted her to see, namely their show-pieces, the things of which they can be proud. Today in most African and Asian countries there are magnificent new hospitals and schools, universities and technical colleges. There are some very wealthy Africans and Asians with fine houses and huge cars. Sometimes they give splendid parties with an air of display seldom found, at least among missionary supporters, in the West. If English tourists stay in one of the few hotels available for foreign visitors, these are the sights they will see in the centre of a capital city and these are the people they will meet. Many of the Africans, moreover, will be *nouveaux riches*. And after a few such encounters a myth is exploded; one more person awakes to a disconcerting reality from a rather pleasant dream in which she (or he) had played a semi-heroic part by being good and dutiful, supporting missions. What can be said about all this?

First, it is entirely natural that new countries should want new buildings. Europeans are hardly in a position to grudge them these. Many of them are erected for prestige purposes; so they often include new airport terminals and government offices and perhaps a skyscraper or two. It takes little imagination to realize that a new country is anxious to make an impression and to put on a good front. In any case all such buildings have been erected at government expense or as a result of foreign aid, not of missionary funds.

But if a sense of proportion is retained by the visitor, it will soon be discovered that such impressive buildings are relatively few, compared with those in most western cities. Moreover the prestige buildings cover up a great deal of poverty. It is at this point that the westerner must try to understand sympathetically, for he is faced with a contradiction. On the one hand a patriotic African will want to show the visitor the things he is proud of, the things that identify Africa with the modern world. He is not likely to conduct the average tourist round the city slums or to show him the more primitive sides of village life. Many an African is indignant when a journalist or a photographer concentrates on the primitive and the backward in reporting or filming his country. But this is understandable enough. Most Britishers would not be very pleased if the main stories and pictures about Britain concentrated on bad housing conditions in Leeds or Glasgow and the seamier sides of our city life. It would be said that this was not a fair presentation and would create a wrong impression. The African feels likewise. On the other hand Africa *is* poor and in perpetual need of every kind of help, financial, technical, economic, personal. There are many agencies, churches and missionary societies and bodies dedicated to fighting poverty, hunger and disease, which want to present this side of Africa— or Asia—in order to elicit such help, to arouse compassion, and to stir the conscience of the world. The developing countries cannot have it both ways, but they often seem to want to. We must be sympathetic to their natural sensitivities in these respects. But the visitor should not be deceived by surface impressions.

Again, it is true that there are some very wealthy people in most countries, even the poorest. India, for example, still has the poorest people in the world and some of the richest, too. But the proportion may be one Dives to a hundred thousand Lazaruses. If a European visitor merely meets the rich in a series of social functions, this does not mean that there are no poor. Let such a visitor wander the streets and see.

It is also true that many of the rich in these countries are very mean. I have sometimes seen Africans, earning substantial salaries, put a penny in the plate even on Christmas Day.

But are not some of the rich mean in western countries? However, there is more to it than this. In most churches overseas people have been brought up to believe that they will be supported by the West, by the mission of whatever type it is. Their attitude to giving has been largely conditioned by this assumption, and it has not always caught up with their change of situation. Even in England the giving of most Anglicans, for instance, has been nothing like adequate or realistic until the recent stewardship campaigns. Up till then we largely depended on the gifts of the dead to keep the Church solvent. We are not in a position to blame Africans and Asians for not doing what most of us have only just begun to do.

Nevertheless, the most important thing to be said about this attitude is that it betrays a total misunderstanding of the concept of mission. 'Mission is not the kindness of the lucky to the unlucky,' says the Anglican document on Mutual Responsibility and Interdependence, issued by the Toronto Congress in 1963. Mission has constantly suffered from being confused with charity and relief. The motive appealed to has too often been that of compassion rather than obedience or witness. Missions are not another form of slumming—slumming at a distance by a series of substitutes who do the work for us. Human need is not to be measured in terms of income. If history had been otherwise and the countries of Africa and Asia had been rich, while Europe and America were poor, the obligation to mission would have been no less compelling. The rich also need the Gospel of Jesus Christ and the free gift of new life in him. Those who live in Mayfair or make their money on Wall Street are those for whom Christ died and are in equal need of Christian mission. Among the educated and the well-to-do there are needs of another kind than poverty and hunger. All over Africa and Asia there are hundreds of thousands of university students, often living between two worlds, a village past and a scientific present; their situation is schizophrenic, the consequent emotional tension and strain immense. They do not generally need our money; they do need Christ. There are countless business men and civil servants, torn between the temptation to dishonesty and easy gain and

a conscience about integrity. There are the conflicts in family
life all the world over, with the younger generation in revolt
and perhaps two thousand years of culture separating a boy
from his parents. There are the intractable problems of
relationships between those of different tribes or castes or
family groups, when a love affair leaps barriers that have never
been crossed before and a prejudiced tradition tries to bring it
to naught and breaks hearts in doing so. There are the masses
of the disenchanted, who looked for happiness and opportunity in their newly independent countries, when the rule of
the foreign imperialist was removed, but have found neither;
and they live without roots and without religion and without
hope—and they exist in every country. None of the millions
represented by these groups can be sufficiently helped by
money alone, and some have no need of money at all. Their
problems will be met only on a quite different level, as were
those of a lame beggar long ago. 'I have no silver or gold, but
what I have I give you, in the name of Jesus Christ of Nazareth,
walk' (Acts 3.6). The Church is engaging in mission only when
in a great variety of situations there are those who can say
some such word as this.

It is not being suggested that money does not matter. Money
is needed on an enormous scale. It is a Christian duty to raise
and give money to the needy millions, and organizations such
as Oxfam and Christian Aid are doing this superbly. It is a
profoundly Christian thing to do. *But this is not mission*. The
discharge of mission requires money to support it, because it
depends on living agents. But mission is not the same as knit-
ting clothes and providing money. The sooner this myth is
exploded and disposed of, the better will be the chance for
church people to discover what mission really is.

THE DILEMMA OF THE MODERN
MISSIONARY

It is easier to caricature and criticize the modern missionary
than to understand him. Since the former Belgian Congo became independent in 1960 nearly a hundred missionaries,

Protestant and Roman Catholic, have met their death serving its peoples. Such men and women do not die for nothing. Someone, commenting on this, said: 'They were killed because they were white; they died because they were Christians.' There, in a word, is part of the dilemma of the modern missionary.

There has been far too little recognition that the changes in the political shape and colour of the world have profoundly affected the position of missionaries. Once the missionary was a key figure because he was foreign, often a member of the ruling European race; now he is a marked man because he belongs to the race that formerly ruled. Once the missionary was popular and highly respected because he brought with him western ways, a new and more powerful magic; now he is often despised or suspect because what he represents has been largely rejected and his motives for being there at all are questioned. Once the missionary had complete freedom of initiative and nothing but nature or hostile men could stand in his way; now the missionary has little or no initiative and he has to fit into a prescribed pattern or go home. Once the missionary was needed, wanted and welcomed; now in many places he is only needed. Once the missionary was invariably in the lead or in junior partnership to other missionaries who held final responsibility; now the missionary is seldom in the lead, often working under nationals of the country and church in which he serves, nationals who may have qualifications much lower than his own, very different ways of doing things and a different set of priorities.

Everyone who goes to another land and people as a missionary is entering into this kind of dilemma. In earlier generations to serve overseas involved great dangers to physical health. Now there is little risk to health but the dangers are psychological and spiritual. Not everyone can take it. The problem is focused in the quotation at the beginning of the chapter, where an educational missionary sees himself as valued in so far as he does a job in the school, a job which is open to him only because not enough Africans are yet qualified for it, but sees also that he is hardly in a position to do anything extra on his own personal initiative by way of evangelism. This is

the heart of the missionary dilemma today. For evangelism
depends on scope for personal initiative. Where this is not
permitted, evangelism is to a great extent restricted. At one
time a missionary had much greater scope for evangelistic
initiative overseas than at home. Today the reverse is true, and
many a young man sees clearly that he will have much greater
freedom of Christian initiative if he remains at home, working
in industry or teaching in a secondary modern school or offering for the probation service, than by being hemmed in and
misunderstood on a highly sensitive staff somewhere in Africa.
He will be right, of course, in recognizing that service in
Africa and Asia may have severe limitations, though the situation in this respect varies a great deal with local conditions;
he will not be right in concluding too quickly that he cannot
exercise any Christian vocation in a situation which limits his
freedom of scope.

Yet another aspect of the missionary's dilemma is the perpetual doubt cast on the sincerity of his motives. What was
expressed so forcibly by the young Indian in the fourth of our
opening quotations was no isolated or exceptional sentiment.
Precisely the same views have been voiced in my hearing by
Christians of different races in countries far apart. The missionary vocation is a permanent invitation to misunderstanding. To be misunderstood by those you have gone to serve is
a much harder cross to bear than to be caricatured by the
cynics in the homeland you have left behind. Today the
presence of the missionary is as often as not resented—not by
the enemies of the Cross of Christ—but by his fellow-
Christians. Sometimes these are clergy.

There is a complex of reasons for this. Some, of course,
result from the missionary's whiteness and the fact that he
comes from a West with an imperial past, still not forgotten,
and from lands which still dominate most of the world's
economy. It is understandable that the have-nots should resent
the haves, though the irony is that many missionaries in fact
have far less of this world's goods than some of the have-nots
whom they serve. Another reason is that the missionary, by
virtue of his education and background, will often have a

much higher degree of competence and efficiency than many of his African or Asian colleagues or superiors. Such an advantage these days is fatal in churches and countries with the first generation of nationals in control. None of us welcomes the presence of those who, even if unconsciously and unwittingly, show up our deficiencies. But most seriously of all, there has been an almost total failure on the part of all but a few of the leaders of the younger churches to understand the inwardness of the missionary calling, as it has presented itself to hundreds of young men and women from Britain, Europe, North America and Australasia. Whatever strains there may have been in relationships, whatever mistakes missionaries may have made, whatever wrong-headedness they may have shown, the fact that most of them became missionaries was the result of an inward call and their motive was a genuine desire to serve.

It is hardly appropriate these days to speak of the *sacrifice* of the missionary vocation, for others also make sacrifices, and the physical hardships, as we have said, are much less than in an earlier age. But there is an inwardness about the missionary call, which comes to many unexpectedly and with a compulsiveness they cannot resist. To answer that call requires certain acts of renunciation and the setting out on an unknown path. There are some in the younger churches who have themselves made costly acts of renunciation, especially those with a higher education who have offered for the ordained ministry as pastors. In Asia there are some who have themselves gone as missionaries to other lands—about two hundred of them. But as yet there are relatively very few indeed in the younger churches who have had any experience comparable to the call that makes a man or woman into a missionary. Among Protestants this has been the nearest equivalent to the call of the cloister in the Roman Catholic and Orthodox Churches. It has involved a degree of obedience, abandonment and permanence not normally required of others. Because of the many unfortunate associations the Christian Mission still has in the minds of Africans and Asians—even Christians, even clergy—there has been virtually no just recognition of the true meaning of the missionary vocation. No missionary is entitled to wish for gratitude—Jesus got none. But the almost universal failure to understand the purity of the missionary's motives at their best and the disinterestedness of his calling makes his position and his acceptability much more difficult today.

Africa and Asia are not quite in step at this point. The crucial year for Asia was 1947 when India became independent; the crucial year for Africa was 1960 when sixteen of its countries became independent. Something of the significance of this thirteen-year time lag is now becoming apparent. In the early 1950s there was a good deal of discussion about the future of missionaries in India and whether there was any need for them. At that stage they were still being associated emotionally with imperial rule and were therefore often resented. By 1961 the situation had changed remarkably. A consultation was held by the National Christian Council of India on 'The Role of the Missionary in India Today'. The Findings wisely insist on safeguarding the full responsibility of Indians for their Church, but among other things they state that:

> It is generally agreed that [foreign] missionaries are still needed in India. The need for missionaries will always exist, since the role of the missionary is not a static one but evolves in relation to the changing historical situation. Even if the practical need for missionary personnel should be less acute, missionaries will still be needed to express the universal and ecumenical character of the Church of God. But at the present time there is still need for missionaries to help the Church in India to fulfil its enormous unfinished talk in its witness to the Lordship of Christ in every area of life.

The Findings also point out that 'Normally a missionary should be ready for a long term commitment to the work of the Church in India.'

Africa today is in much the same position and mood as India was in the 1950s. Not only is the desirability of any missionary presence being questioned, but in public utterances many Christian African leaders are being extremely critical of missionaries. They had a good opportunity for doing this at the First All Africa Conference of Churches held at Kampala, Uganda, in April 1963, and they took it. A distinguished Asian Christian, D. T. Niles of Ceylon, who was present at the conference, has made this comment :

> I sensed that emotions were still too much generated by a past that is gone. A casual observer from outside cannot easily gauge the extent to which the past is gone, for, while legally and administratively things may have changed, it is still possible that in the actual circumstances of people's lives the old still remains. Nevertheless, the tasks of the future demand that the emotional strength of the Church should be harnessed to the future.[1]

These remarks from Asia provide a useful corrective both for the Africans and the missionaries. It is important that the African church leaders should turn their attention to the future instead of indulging in constant recrimination about the past. But it is also important that so long as they feel bitter and angry they should express this. In the meanwhile the missionaries must be big enough to take it, realizing not only the strong psychological pressures behind it all but accepting it as a judgment which our generation must bear for the sins and shortcomings of our forefathers, and asking, 'Lord, is it I?'

It is within this context of frustration and misunderstanding, of doing the unspectacular things that others do not want to do, that the modern missionary gives his witness and makes his contribution. The main characteristics of this context may not change for some time; Africa has much for which to forgive the West, as the deaths in the Congo testify. Perhaps after a few years the situation will change for the better, as it has done in India. The probability is that the period of adjustment will take rather longer, for there is a greater back-log of hatred and resentment in Africa than there was in India and long centuries of the slave trade to which India was never subject. The best type of missionary will accept all this and put up with what seems painful and unfair. But the best type of missionary will also want to have the opportunity to lead

[1] *International Review of Missions*, Oct. 1963, Vol. LII, No. 208, p. 410.

people to a knowledge of Jesus Christ. This is the passionate desire that makes the missionary and sends him to the ends of the earth. And this is the heart of his present dilemma. Any missionary in the true apostolic succession will be ready to suffer for Christ's sake and the Gospel's. The hardest thing of all for him to bear is the curtailment of evangelistic initiative, referred to in the letter cited at the beginning, because of its implied criticism of the African *status quo*.

If we are to feel with the missionary here we have to remember that very often it is the Christian Church, not some non-Christian state or institution, which deprives him of such initiative. This is what is new in the modern situation. It is this that doubles the frustration.

> It is not an enemy who taunts me—then I could bear it; it is not an adversary who deals insolently with me—then I could hide from him. But it is you, my equal, my familiar friend. We used to hold sweet converse together; within God's house we walked in fellowship (Ps. 55.12-14 RSV).

How aptly these ancient words describe what many a former missionary in China must feel as he reads what Chinese Christians have said about missionaries since 1949. The same words express the feelings of missionaries elsewhere, still in the thick of it all.

Once again it is from Asia that light is beginning to shine on this problem, possibly because Asia is just that much further away from the colonial era than Africa and many of its Churches have been autonomous for longer. In an unpublished address given in 1964 D. T. Niles, himself a leader of a younger Church, urged that missionary societies should once again be in a position to take their own initiatives. Speaking to a group of missionary executives in one such society he said: 'During the period when authority was being transferred to the Churches in Asia you had a glorious fifteen years of irresponsibility. We made all the decisions; you simply wrote the cheques. *Now that must stop.* You must have a set-up whereby you are knowledgeable, whereby you can make up your mind as to what are the right things to do, and then really push.'

That is a frank plea for a recovery of missionary initiative, and with it was joined an equally strong plea for more 'old-time missionaries'. This expression does not mean missionaries who rule but missionaries who belong and who remain for a number of years. 'We are not looking merely for fraternal helpers. We want missionaries. We know that you cannot find too many of them, but at least send us some. I am not against fraternal helpers. I am only protesting that they are not missionaries. They are helpers. We need any amount of help, but it is the missionary that is wanted, and wanted badly.' Such words from one of Asia's most outstanding Christians do not require comment, and they serve as a salutary corrective to some of the nonsense that has been written recently about the day of the missionary being over.

We must be prepared then for the missionary's dilemma to be a continual factor for most of this generation. At the same time we should notice that this dilemma only arises in situations where missions have had some success. It is felt most acutely where the mission has partially achieved its first objective in building up an indigenous Church. Where there is no indigenous Church to speak of and the Mission is still largely in control there is of course no such dilemma. For example, Anglican missions in Argentina and Chile have not yet produced an indigenous Church of any size; the missionary therefore still has considerable powers of initiative and control and has not yet experienced this kind of problem. (Undoubtedly this is one reason why the continent of South America holds out so strong an appeal to a certain type of missionary recruit who does not want to be thwarted in his evangelism by an indigenous Church which may wish him to do other things.) On the other hand Episcopalian missions from the United States to Brazil have been able to implant an indigenous Church there, with the result that some American missionaries now find themselves in this dilemma. In East and West Africa, as in India, Pakistan and Japan, Anglican, Methodist and Presbyterian missions have produced Churches which are now to a great extent indigenous, and in which missionaries therefore increasingly feel the tension during this stage immediately after the transference of power. But some of the inter-denominational societies, especially those from North America, have not yet created indigenous and autonomous Churches, so their missionaries are still free from the strains of this situation.

Part of the trouble comes from a wild mishandling of certain courageous phrases coined in the last century. One of the most famous was 'the euthanasia of the Mission', used by Henry Venn, Secretary of the Church Missionary Society from 1841 to 1872. The euthanasia of the Mission meant its making way for a self-supporting, self-governing, self-extending native Church. It never meant the euthanasia of the missionary; nor did it mean the euthanasia of mission, as distinct from the Mission. What Venn had in mind was the Mission as a power-structure, with all the inherent dangers of paternalism. His vision was of the day when the missionary would resign his superintendence and control, transferring this to the native Church, and making himself dispensable *in this way*. He did not envisage the resignation of the missionary's control as his disappearance altogether or as making him redundant. The missionary and the missionary agency would then move on to the new unevangelized fields.[1] Unless one interprets this last phrase in strictly geographical terms, there are more of these today than ever, vast areas of life—and, incidentally of land—where no indigenous Church is having any influence whatsoever. Venn's great aim was for missionary mobility and flexibility. He never contemplated missionaries being confined to institutions, as many Churches today confine them, but a limiting of themselves to evangelistic work and a refusal to be involved in church administration, once the Church is established. What D. T. Niles is asking for is a good deal near to all that was in Venn's mind. Until something of this is grasped by the churches—and by all missionaries—the missionary's dilemma will remain.[2]

[1] For a criticism of Venn's view see Stephen Neill, *A History of Christian Missions*, Penguin Books 1964, 260.
[2] A useful discussion of Venn's theory will be found in Peter Beyerhaus and Henry Lefever, *The Responsible Church and the Foreign Mission*, World Dominion Press 1964, pp. 25-30.

THE MEASUREMENT OF FAILURE
AND SUCCESS

'The attempt to conquer Asia for Christ has definitely failed,' wrote K. M. Panikkar. 'The kingdom of the world has become the kingdom of our Lord and of his Christ, and he shall reign for ever and ever' (Rev. 11.15 RSV), says the angel in the Apocalypse. The first statement is empirical, the second prophetic. Terms like failure and success are purely relative and cannot be suitably applied to the Christian Mission, because its effectiveness cannot be assessed at any given moment of time but only at the End. In a later chapter we shall consider the final goal of the Christian mission from a theological point of view. Here our concern is to face up to what looks like present failure in at least some respects, a failure which is disturbing partly because it contributes to the misunderstanding of mission.

There is no command in the New Testament that Christians are to convert everyone. Nor is there any promise that the world will itself be converted. The command to Christians is to bear witness to Jesus Christ (Acts 1.8; Luke 24.48) and to 'make disciples of all nations'.[1] The promise is that the end comes, when Christ 'delivers up the kingdom to God the Father, after abolishing every kind of domination, authority, and power. For he is destined to reign until God has put all enemies under his feet' (I Cor. 15.24, 25). Other books of the New Testament have variant forms of this same promise and hope of God's final triumph. There is nothing to suggest that as a result of the Christian mission the whole world will eventually become Christian. The Church in its mission will receive the same responses as Christ in his, allegiance and opposition, and there is no reason for expecting that it will have more 'success'. For ours is not a separate and distinctive mission. 'This mission is Christ's.'[2] This means that there is

[1] Matt. 28.19, of which a very thorough exegesis by Karl Barth may be found in Gerald H. Anderson (ed.), *The Theology of the Christian Mission*, SCM Press 1961, 63ff.

[2] See the important chapter 6, bearing this title, in R. K. Orchard, *Missions in a Time of Testing*, Lutterworth 1964.

B

always a double paradox about the Christian mission. First, it is
completed from the beginning. Second, its success is seen in
and arises from its apparent failure.

We must look at these two propositions. God's mission to
man was completed in principle in Jesus Christ. Nothing the
Church can do can add to his finished redeeming work. The
Church does not take Christ to places where he is not already;
he takes the Church to places where it is not already. The
Church does not initiate or bring the reign of God in different
societies; the most it can do is to bear witness to that reign
and make it visible in its own life. This has been admirably
put by R. K. Orchard:

> The Christian mission . . . is to affirm both God's reign and
> the offer of participation through Christ in that reign. This is
> not to say that the reign of God is present only where the mission
> is, or to confine his Kingdom to those times and places where it
> becomes articulate through mission. That would be to make God
> subject to his witnesses, and to testify not to the Lord of all,
> but to a tribal Baal. . . . God's reign is over all, and is not
> dependent on human testimony to it.[1]

Orchard goes on to argue that one consequence of affirming
that the Mission is Christ's before it is ours is to prevent our
identifying the churches with the Kingdom of God.

> To make that identification is to make Christ the prisoner of his
> witnesses. . . . He is Lord over them, not subject to them. They
> are witnesses to him, not proprietors of him.[2]

We cannot therefore speak of mission in terms of success or
failure if these are measured in statistics of conversions, for
there is no guarantee tied in with the original Gospel that all
or most will respond in this world and in this life. This means
that K. M. Panikkar is no more justified in writing of the
failure of the Church's mission in Asia after four hundred
years than is Nicolas Stacey in deploring the failure of the
Church's mission in Woolwich after four years of special effort

[1] Op. cit., 73.   [2] Ibid., 75.

by a gifted team. We can speak of the success or failure of mission only in terms of witness and obedience, not of results.

This brings us to the second paradox, namely that what looks like failure may be success. When Jesus died on Calvary there was little to show by way of visible results; the whole picture looked like failure. But he was offering to God in a final sacrifice a life in which his witness and obedience to his Father had been perfect. The world's salvation resulted from that perfection of obedience, not from the number of disciples at the close of the Lord's earthly ministry. It was this that constituted the completeness of his mission in God's eyes, even though there was little visible to show for it in men's eyes. The lowest point of apparent failure had been reached, the rejection which was death on a cross.

> *Therefore* God has highly exalted him and bestowed on him the name which is above every name, that at the name of Jesus every knee should bow, in heaven and on earth and under the earth, and every tongue confess that Jesus Christ is Lord, to the glory of God the Father (Phil. 2.8-11 RSV).

Jesus achieved what he was sent to do because he was not concerned with the categories of success and failure as understood by the world. Because he was content to appear to fail in the sight of men, if this had to be the cost of witness to the truth and obedience to God, his mission gained an effectiveness which became universal. There is reason to suppose that the pattern of the Church's mission, at least in some countries, may not be altogether dissimilar. It could at one and the same time seem to be a total failure in the eyes of men and yet, by its faithfulness in obedience and witness, be the means of achieving God's will ultimately in those countries. Because 'the Lord sees not as man sees' (I Sam. 16.7) it is wise for Christians to regard no one and no situation merely from a human point of view (II Cor. 5.16 RSV).

If we begin to measure the Church's success and failure in terms of obedience rather than results a very different picture emerges. Some of the larger Churches with a considerable membership would perhaps be found rather low in any list,

while some of the smallest Churches, making very few converts, would rank high. (For a further consideration of this
point see chapter 3.) The point to grasp is that although a
church is not a failure if it does not succeed in making converts, it is a failure if it has ceased to bear witness and no
longer attempts to make converts. A Roman Catholic missionary scholar in Uganda has written some words which most of
us could endorse.

> It is not the number of baptized that indicates the success of
> a foreign mission, but the growth of those who are baptized into
> a full Christian life which necessarily involves giving as well
> as receiving, participation in the apostolate and not merely being
> preached to. The real crown of a mission is the entry of the new
> Church herself into the missionary apostolate; when she herself
> sends her children away to preach the faith, then, and not until
> then, has she reached ecclesial adulthood. It is that at which the
> foreign missionary must aim from the very first, it is more fruit-
> ful to baptize a nucleus and develop the ministry, than to bring
> in thousands but develop a habit of Christian dependence on a
> foreign missionary which cannot later be easily broken. The
> foreign missionary is not meant to convert a country, that is for
> the home missionary. The foreign missionary's job is to create a
> cell which will then evangelize a society from within.[1]

In many countries today the Church is little more than such a
cell, but wherever such a cell exists for witness and lives obe-
diently, no one is entitled to speak of the Christian mission's
failure.

This must not be taken to mean that the Church can be
complacent about lack of converts and lack of growth. A
Church which is alive normally grows. If there is no growth or
expansion questions must be asked and reasons sought. Sometimes failure is the result of wrong policy or out-dated methods.
A study of religious sociology and its application to particular
areas may be essential for the reversal of some unnecessary
failures. It is outside the scope of this chapter to assess sociology other than to note its importance for analysis rather

  [1] Adrian Hastings, *The World Mission of the Church*, Darton, Long-
man and Todd 1964, 46.

than cure. It is likewise beyond our scope to discuss the social effects of the Christian mission, which have been enormous in Africa, India and the Pacific Islands, even when converts have been disappointingly few. Bishop Stephen Neill is prepared to accept much of the criticism Panikkar levels against missions in Asia, but he adds :

He hardly does justice to the immense influence that the Gospel has exercised far beyond the limits of the organized Church; the Indian revolution, of which Mr Panikkar himself is a champion, would be unthinkable without the influence of the New Testament on Māhatma Gāndhi.[1]

In Africa also the effect of missions socially and politically is incalculable. It is impossible to conceive of Africa as it is today, throbbing with energy and life, apart from the missionary enterprise, and no great African country has reached its independence without a generous tribute being paid by African leaders to what the missionaries have done in preparing the way. Certainly this is an outcome very different from that expected by some of the missionaries. But if God is in control of history we may not doubt that this was part of his purpose. Whatever has contributed to this cannot be written off as failure.

The End may be near or far, but it is not yet in sight. We cannot guess the shape of things to come or trace the curves of the Church's prospective success and failure in the future. The best short appraisal of the present position of Christianity across the world will be found in the concluding chapter of Bishop Stephen Neill's *History of Christian Missions*. He asserts that 'the age of missions is at an end; the age of mission has begun'.[2] In effect this means that no longer can missions be a *department* of the Churches' life but their central and predominant concern, every committed adult Christian seeking his own vocation and ministry within the one supreme calling

[1] Stephen Neill, op. cit., 56. A valuable discussion will be found in Norman Goodall, *Christian Missions and Social Ferment*, Epworth Press 1964.
[2] Page 572.

of the Church to make Christ fully known in all the world. Those who are committed to this task, however humbly, will find themselves too preoccupied with the many kinds of witness and service they do for Christ's sake to be unduly put off by the accusation of failure, or puffed up by the taste of success. Perhaps St Paul was implying this when he wrote:

> But with me it is a very small thing that I should be judged by you or by any human court. I do not even judge myself. I am not aware of anything against myself, but I am not thereby acquitted. It is the Lord who judges me. Therefore do not pronounce judgment before the time, before the Lord comes, who will bring to light the things now hidden in darkness and will disclose the purposes of the heart (I Cor. 4.3-5 RSV).

Those words were written in a missionary context, emphasizing the fundamental requirement of faithfulness.

2

MEANINGS OF MISSION
Towards a Theology

THE New Testament does not give a neat definition of mission. Instead it presents us with a missionary God and a missionary Church. It is the nature of God that makes the Church missionary. The Church's mission is derived from—and in some sense continuous with—the mission of the Divine Son. 'As the Father has sent me, even so I send you' (John 20.21). Mission describes the great sending movement of God, in Christ and through his Church, to the world he loves. One who is 'sent' is an apostle or missionary. What he is sent to do or discharge is his 'mission'. Today mission and missionary can both be used in a purely secular sense. In Christian usage the sender is always God; the one sent is his messenger, his servant, his representative; and the mission itself is God's business, his work.

The word 'apostle' occurs more than eighty times in the New Testament. In most instances it means an apostle of Jesus Christ, one sent by him. In one notable case it is applied to Jesus himself, 'the apostle and high priest of our confession' (Heb. 3.1). Jesus was the first apostle; he is the chief apostle. The Christian mission originates in him, as he originates in God. The mission of the Church can therefore be said to mean its doing that which makes it apostolic.

What is that?

Because the New Testament prefers images and illustrations to definitions, this question cannot be answered in a word. Moreover, mission has many facets. In this chapter we will look at seven concepts, each of which sums up one cluster of ideas about the Church's mission as it is set out in the New

Testament. These are: Affirmation, Proclamation, Subordination, Penetration, Mediation, Integration, Consummation.

MISSION AS AFFIRMATION

The Church is called to be an affirming community. It says:
God is love; Jesus is Lord; Christ died for our sins. If the Church
can no longer make these affirmations it forfeits its claim to be
recognized as the Church of Jesus Christ. An affirmation is a
positive statement, asserted with strong conviction. An affirmative means answering yes. The Christian Gospel is both
these things. It is God's affirmation about himself in Jesus
Christ. It is God's affirmative to men in Jesus Christ.

> The language in which we address you is not an ambiguous
> blend of Yes and No. The Son of God, Christ Jesus, proclaimed
> among you by us . . . was never a blend of Yes and No. With
> him it was, and is, Yes. He is the Yes pronounced upon God's
> promises, every one of them. That is why, when we give glory
> to God, it is through Christ Jesus that we say 'Amen' (II Cor,
> 1.18-20).

This passage is, of course, an inspired aside. Paul was dealing
with an accusation the Corinthian Christians had levelled
against him, that he had changed his mind about a visit, first
saying Yes and then No. Suddenly the apostle darts off into a
digression in which he says that there is nothing equivocal
about the Christian message, the Gospel, nor about Jesus Christ
himself. The Gospel is a positive affirmation. It is God saying
Yes to men in Jesus Christ. Christ is the Yes. In him God meets
all the basic needs of our existence affirmatively. So Paul
lights upon one of the greatest and most original titles given
to Jesus in the New Testament—the Yes.

On what grounds can he make this assertion? Evidently Paul
knew enough about the human life of Jesus to regard him as
the supreme affirmative. This aspect of the Lord is clearly
presented in all four gospels. We find it illustrated in his attitude to ordinary people and to the multitude as a whole. The
multitude, typifying mass man in most ages, was conditioned
by a series of negatives. To most of its greatest longings and

deepest needs it had become accustomed to expecting the answer No. In normal circumstances there was no way of deliverance from disease, hunger, and death, man's three basic problems. Even religion had little to offer except consolation and possibly hope. It could not provide healing, food, and life. The New Testament portrays religion, that of Judaism, as impotent in the face of man's real needs. It has no immediately affirmative answer. But what was so startlingly new about Jesus was that in precisely the same situations where all other men, all other religions, would have said No—there is nothing we can do—he said Yes. The gospels provide illustrations of this from each of these three areas of the human condition.

First, disease. Two examples will be sufficient to make the point. They can be seen in the first two acts of healing recorded by Matthew (8.1-13).

> And now a leper approached him, bowed low, and said, 'Sir, if only you will, you can cleanse me.' Jesus stretched out his hand, touched him, and said, 'Indeed I will; be clean again.' And his leprosy was cured immediately.

There is no equivocation. Jesus says the strongest possible Yes to the diseased man's request. We are told nothing about his spiritual condition. The story portrays, among other things, God's affirmative attitude towards the healing of disease.

> When he had entered Capernaum a centurion came up to ask his help. 'Sir,' he said, 'a boy of mine lies at home paralysed and racked with pain.' Jesus said, 'I will come and cure him.'

Once again there is no equivocation, no blend of Yes and No, no ambiguity or uncertainty. The need is stated and the answer is given—in affirmative language. The great Yes of divine compassion and healing power was being uttered in the actual ministry of Jesus Christ. In him the Old Testament promises about the blind seeing and the lame walking in the day of the Lord, the Messianic age, were coming true before men's eyes. He is the Yes.

Secondly, hunger. The gospel narratives record two distinct

feedings of the multitude. We will look at one only, as described by Mark (6.34-44).

> When he came ashore, he saw a great crowd and his heart went out to them, because they were like sheep without a shepherd; and he had much to teach them. As the day wore on, his disciples approached him and said, 'This is a lonely place and it is getting very late; send the people off to the farms and villages round about, to buy themselves something to eat.' 'Give them something to eat yourselves', he answered. They replied, 'Are we to go and spend twenty pounds on bread to give them a meal?' 'How many loaves have you?' he asked; 'go and see.' They found out and told him, 'Five, and two fishes also.' He ordered them to make the people sit down in groups on the green grass, and they sat down in rows, a hundred rows of fifty each. Then, taking the five loaves and the two fishes, he looked up to heaven, said the blessing, broke the loaves, and gave them to the disciples to distribute. He also divided the two fishes among them. They all ate to their hearts' content and twelve basketfuls of scraps were picked up, with what was left of the fish. Those who ate the loaves numbered five thousand men.

It is not necessary to expound this story in full, for we need notice only those of its aspects which reveal Jesus as God's Yes. We are introduced to a crisis-situation. There is a tired and hungry crowd, but there is no food. The disciples react negatively. 'Send them away. We cannot do anything. This is too big for us.' In other words, to a condition of human need they can say nothing but No. (This has often been the attitude of the Church through the centuries in similar situations of overwhelming challenge and need.) But Jesus will not allow this. He tells them, in effect, to say Yes. 'You give them something to eat yourselves.' They prevaricate with their further question, intended to show the absurdity as well as the enormity of his suggestion. He still insists on saying Yes, doing so in faith, using the slender resources available, five loaves and two fishes. The Church has to learn that its supreme asset does not lie in its material possessions and its own resources but in its Lord. He can say Yes. He wants to feed the multitude, to feed mankind, and he does so. There is a lot left over.

> high Heaven rejects the lore
> Of nicely-calculated less or more. . . .

The Old Testament promises about feasting, a time of plenty,
are fulfilled (e.g. Isa. 25.6). He is the Yes.

Thirdly, death. There are three deaths in the gospels: Jairus's
daughter, the son of the widow of Nain, and Lazarus. In each
case Jesus says Yes to the plea, spoken or unspoken, for deliverance, but the last is the most dramatic. The grave of
Lazarus symbolizes the final negative of death. Jesus, however,
on hearing the news, makes his ultimate affirmation, 'I am the
resurrection and I am life' (John 11.25). Because of his very
being he can affirm life in the presence of death and so command death itself and conquer it.

> 'Lazarus, come forth.' The dead man came out, his hands and
> feet swathed in linen bands, his face wrapped in a cloth. Jesus
> said, 'Loose him; let him go' (John 11.43, 44).

He is the Yes. The Old Testament yearnings for the breaking of
death's hold on man find their fulfilment in Jesus Christ.

It is possible to work through the gospels tracing this
theology of affirmation. We have concentrated on three areas
of deeply felt human need. There are others, one of the most
recurrent, though more specifically religious, being the need
for forgiveness. Often this was inarticulate, perhaps even
unconscious. But to a paralysed man Jesus could say, 'My son,
your sins are forgiven', and to a woman of the streets 'Your sins
are forgiven' (Mark 2.5; Luke 7.49). In all these spheres of life,
sickness, hunger, death, sin, Jesus speaks and acts affirmatively.
Mission is the continuance of those affirmatives in a world
where, despite all other change, man's basic needs remain un-
changing. Being the guardian of a Gospel with such wide
affirmations about God's will for mankind, the Church cannot
avoid the social and psychological and economic implications
of that Gospel. At some times and in some places the discharge of its mission will involve the Church still in feeding
the hungry and healing the sick. But in doing this the Church
must not forget that man does not live by bread alone and that

sickness usually extends far beyond the physical and far beyond the individual.

But we have not done with the theology of affirmation. It is
a two-way matter. For the fundamental affirmation which
Jesus made was on Calvary. There he said the all-embracing
Yes with his whole life offered to his Father. The Gethsemane
prayer, 'Not what I will, but what thou wilt', was being
worked out on the Cross. A later passage in the New Testament
itself provides the best commentary on these words.

> When Christ came into the world, he said, 'Sacrifices and
> offerings thou hast not desired, but a body hast thou prepared
> for me; in burnt offerings and sin offerings thou hast taken no
> pleasure. Then I said, "Lo, I have come to do thy will, O God,"
> as it is written of me in the roll of the book.' . . . And by that
> will we have been sanctified through the offering of the body
> of Christ once for all (Heb. 10.5-7, 10 RSV).

In Jesus God said Yes to man. In Jesus man also said Yes, for
the first time perfectly, to God. And Jesus said Yes to God
in situations where most other men would have said No. It was
his Yes of acceptance at the point of death and sacrifice, cruel
and unjust, which achieved the salvation of the world. By all
that followed from this affirmation, once made in history, in
man and for man, the new humanity was created, the
humanity in which God's promises could begin to be fulfilled
and his will worked out.

But this Godward Yes has to be reiterated by the Church.
Paul saw this clearly when he added, 'That is why, when we
give glory to God, it is through Christ Jesus that we say
"Amen".' Christianity is more than Christ saying Yes to God
and Yes to men. It is also men saying Yes to Jesus Christ.
'Amen' is another form of Yes; it is an expression of agreement
equivalent to our 'certainly' or 'of course'. The dual affirmation
of Jesus to God and men, which was the very meaning of his
existence and is the *esse* of the Gospel itself, therefore provides
part of the theological basis for the Christian mission. But that
mission continues only in so far as the Church continues to
say Yes with Christ and to Christ in a vast assortment of

situations. For the *raison d'être* of the Church is to be the Body of Christ in which he goes on saying his dual Yes through all the centuries and until history ends. So the Church does this —to God in obedience and worship, to men in evangelism and service. In a world of immense need, to recapture the concept of an affirming Church would do much to make both it and the Christian message more relevant.

MISSION AS PROCLAMATION

That which the Church affirms it must also proclaim. The creeds, which state some of the Christian affirmations in theological language, ought, if properly understood, to provide a compelling impetus for mission. When the truth of some great scientific discovery has been verified and affirmed within the nucleus of those who know, it is forthwith proclaimed to the world at large that all may benefit. It becomes news.

Today the Gospel is so old that it is hard for us to imagine the reactions of those first hearers to whom it came as news. Missionaries proclaiming it to peoples who have never heard it before come nearest to the experience. There are indications that soon, perhaps, in a generation or two, it will again become news in the West.[1]

The New Testament uses three sets of words for proclamation or preaching: *euangelizesthai*, to preach good tidings; *katangellein*, to make an announcement or declaration, *kērussein*, to proclaim as a herald. Of these the second is the weakest and most matter-of-fact; the first suggests telling something to people who have not heard it before; the third implies a sense of solemnity and importance and wonder, for it is 'a proclamation made by a herald, by the town-crier, in the full light of day, to the sound of a trumpet, up-to-the-minute, addressed to everyone because it comes from the king himself'.[2] In our time news-items of such significance are 'proclaimed'

[1] Cf. 'I know no group more ready to be evangelized than young intellectuals'. A. C. Bridge in *Mission and Communication*, ed. D. M. Paton, SPCK 1963, 82.

[2] *Vocabulary of the Bible*, ed. by J.-J. von Allmen, Lutterworth 1958, art. *Preaching*.

by the mass communication media, press, radio, and television.
The idea remains the same; the difference is in the means of
communication and their speed. In fact the word 'communication' might almost be used as a synonym for 'proclamation'
as we are interpreting it. For 'proclamation' has always been
something much bigger than the mere delivery of sermons—as
has preaching. Mission means the perpetual communication
of Jesus Christ by the Church to the world, the perpetual
interpretation of Christ, retrieving him from the misrepresenta-
tion of theological systems, the limitations of denominations,
and the distortion of institutional Christianity.

The original Christian proclamation was made by Jesus
himself. 'Jesus came into Galilee proclaiming (*kērussōn*) the
Gospel of God: "The time has come; the kingdom of God is
upon you; repent, and believe the Gospel"' (Mark 1.14, 15).
After the Resurrection and the gift of the Spirit at Pentecost
Jesus becomes the object of the Church's proclamation.

> 'God has made this Jesus, whom you crucified, both Lord and
> Messiah. . . . This Jesus is the stone rejected by the builders
> which has become the keystone. . . . He it is whom God has
> exalted with his own right hand as leader and Saviour, to grant
> Israel repentance and forgiveness of sins. . . . It is through him
> that forgiveness of sins is now being proclaimed to you' (Acts
> 2.36; 4.11; 5.31; 13.38).

Christian preaching therefore is the proclamation of Christ; he
is its content. 'It is not ourselves that we proclaim; we proclaim Christ Jesus as Lord, and ourselves as your servants, for
Jesus' sake' (II Cor. 4.5). The following comment on this text
is worth quoting:

> The preacher does not preach himself; he is not a virtuoso of
> religion, performing by means of a kind of contagion and im-
> posing his personality upon his audience, but the servant of
> those to whom he speaks for the sake of Jesus.[1]

St Paul's words would also imply that in its mission the Church
does not proclaim a particular orthodoxy or a system of doc-

[1] Art. on *Preaching*, op. cit.

trine or itself; its concern is to present Christ. As the Jerusalem Conference of 1928 said: 'Our message is Jesus Christ; we dare not give less, and we cannot give more.'

The proclamation of Christ as Lord is a positive statement. It contains no direct critique of other religions. For the early Church this lifted the Gospel out of the arena of syncretism or the comparative study of religion. They were not propagating a religious conviction or a spiritual experience, but the news of an event that had really happened, of a man who had really lived, in whom the Kingdom of God had come and for whom no other name would do but Lord. The very nature of Lordship or Kingship demands that it be recognized and therefore proclaimed. In the history of England as soon as one sovereign succeeds on the death of another, he must be proclaimed.

It is in the missionary consciousness of the primitive Church that we see most clearly how completely the faithful were convinced that they had received the one and only revelation, the proclamation of which was a matter of life or death for humanity.[1]

In the New Testament the missionary proclamation is not seen as a matter of choice but rather of obligation and even compulsion. Looked at from the point of view of obedience, the act of proclamation is an obligation; looked at from the point of view of love, it must be regarded as a compulsion. These two approaches are found in St Paul. 'Necessity is laid upon me. Woe to me if I do not preach the Gospel' (I Cor. 9.16 RSV). 'The love of Christ leaves us no choice. . . . We come therefore as Christ's ambassadors. It is as if God were appealing to you through us: in Christ's name, we implore you, be reconciled to God' (II Cor. 5.14, 20). Paul felt that he *owed* the Gospel both to the Barbarian and the Greek, the ignorant and the cultured (Rom. 1.14). The proclamation of the Gospel in mission was part of the very organic life of the apostolic Church. Perhaps the nearest, and not altogether surprising, analogy to this is the sex-instinct. Early in the Bible there is God's command to Noah, 'Be fruitful and multiply,

[1] W. A. Visser 't Hooft, *No Other Name*, SCM Press 1963, 75.

and fill the earth' (Gen. 9.1). To reproduce is a human obligation, a necessity laid upon man. But it has not been unduly
difficult to obey this command, because with it is provided
an instinct of compelling proportions. In the sex-act people
are conscious of yielding to a compulsive force rather than
obeying a primitive injunction. It is the compulsion of love,
the fruit of which is always reproduction. So with the Church,
reproduction and growth are meant to be the result not of a
dogged obedience so much as of an instinctive and compelling
love. 'We cannot but speak of what we have seen and heard'
(Acts 4.20 RSV). There is a naturalness about this kind of
proclamation; it is not forced; it was not self-conscious obedience. It is most unlikely that the first Christians were aware
of the great missionary command as it is formulated at the
end of St Matthew's gospel. They did not preach because they
were told to, but because they wanted to; it was a spontaneous
response to situations of opportunity.

The act of proclaiming can of course take many different
forms; the sermon, the song, the dialogue, the conversation,
the silent witness of Christian integrity, the personal confession of faith in Christ before men, the selfless acts of service
inspired by love for Jesus, the total life and thrust of the
Christian community in a particular place—all these can be
ways of proclaiming Jesus Christ, of communicating something of him, and so engaging in mission at this level.

Like the herald of old, those who preach or communicate
the Gospel of Christ do not act on their own authority but on
that of him who sends them. 'How can men preach *unless they
are sent*?' (Rom. 10.15 RSV). They are spokesmen. They did not
devise the message themselves but received it from their
master. They are not expected to deliver their own ideas and
opinions in the act of proclamation; if they wish to do this
they must seek other occasions. In their mission they are
simply agents. Any claim they have to be taken seriously and
listened to rests not on themselves but solely on the authority
of him who sends them and on the self-authenticating nature
of the message they bear. They function as representatives.

Not everyone is called to be a preacher, though everyone is

called to be a witness. Christ is proclaimed as much by his witnesses as by his servants in pulpits, and often more effectively. But the Church as a community is committed to this task of proclamation.

Much attention is paid today to the techniques of communication, and they are important. But is sufficient attention given to the New Testament teaching about the Holy Spirit as being the true communicator of Jesus Christ? According to the Fourth Gospel communication is a major part of the mission of the Spirit. He is sent in order to teach the disciples all things and to bring to their minds what Jesus had already said, to bear witness to Jesus, to guide them into all the truth, and to make known to them what the Lord continues to say (John 14.26; 15.26; 16.13, 14). He will also *convince* the world (John 16.8-10). No one else can, except by the Spirit's inspiration and aid. He brings to bear, both upon the Church and the world, the truth of God as it is in Jesus.

No perfecting of techniques will be adequate for the task of proclamation in the contemporary world unless these are shot through with the light and truth and power of the Spirit. We see this operating on the Day of Pentecost and in the events recorded in Acts 2. All too often the main point is missed through concentrating on the problem of tongues. What is being conveyed by the account is that there had been real communication, breaking through the language barrier, symbolized by the story of Babel in Genesis 11, which the gift of the Spirit promptly and for the first time surmounts. A great variety of people from many language groups remark that 'we hear them telling in our own tongues the mighty works of God' (Acts 2.11). It is most improbable that the apostles actually spoke in foreign languages, but somehow the message got through. The reason for this is that the Spirit has means of communication at his disposal not open to ordinary men. This is something more than verbal language. Two partial parallels may be seen in the language of love and the language of music. Lovers can convey love without a word being spoken, and two people can love each other and communicate their love when neither knows the other's language. Music, like-

wise, rises over the walls of language by speaking at depths
which words do not reach. It is surely in some such way that
we must conceive of the communication of the Spirit, as he
reminds and teaches, convinces and convicts. Words are not
unimportant but they have their limitations. He can over-
reach these and get through. If this were not so all our attempts
at communicating the Christian Gospel would be vain. Mission
can be by means of proclamation only because the Spirit has
been given to be the driving force behind the words and the
interpreting power within them and those who hear them.

MISSION AS SUBORDINATION

The proclamation of Christ Jesus as Lord has a corollary:
'ourselves your servants for Jesus' sake' (II Cor. 4.5). Servants,
however distinguished, are always subordinates. In another
passage St Paul speaks of missionaries as 'Christ's underlings'
(I Cor. 4.1). The word 'subordination' is used here in preference
to 'service', which has become so common and commercialized
an expression that it has largely lost its real and original meaning. Those engaged in mission are automatically engaged in
ministry of some kind, and to be ministering means to be
subordinate, to be under orders. A deliberate renunciation of
status, especially of power and prestige, is fundamental to the
concept of mission. Today we are seeing this with a new
clarity. Often in the past those engaged in mission have
assumed certain powers by way of right because they were
white or western, and in doing so have gravely obscured and
distorted the meaning of mission. This applies not only to the
individual missionary but to the Church as a whole in many
a missionary situation. 'A privileged Church must be a docile
Church. . . . Every time that the Church in history has
accepted privilege, she has found bondage.'[1] The Anglican
Church in India, the Roman Catholic Church in the Congo, the
Dutch Church in Indonesia, have all suffered by reason of a
privileged relation to the ruling power. The majority of missionaries felt immense relief when, with the coming of political

[1] Adrian Hastings, op. cit., 17, 51.

independence, these privileges were swept away. At last the Christian mission could be seen in its own and not in a borrowed light. Inevitably there must be a time-lag of at least one whole generation before this becomes fully possible. There are, however, still a few pockets of missionaries who expect privilege and protection of a kind unknown by the early Church and who find it hard to give up presupposing and pining for a Christendom which no longer exists.

The imperialism of the European nations in the last four centuries has been neither a total misfortune nor a total blessing. Dr Max Warren has gone so far as to write about 'a theology of imperialism' in an attempt to draw up a balance sheet.[1] We must believe that the God of history was as much responsible for this now closed imperialist chapter, in the last third of which the Christian mission made such progress, as for that earlier imperialism of Rome under which Jesus and his Church were born and reared. But there is this difference: the earlier imperialism was a constant threat to the Church's survival even though it provided the means for its expansion —roads, a common language and the rest. The later imperialism favoured and often used the Church for its own ends and by so doing surrounded the Gospel with a certain ambiguity, thus making Christianity less acceptable now to some of the newly emancipated. The first imperialism began by being secular and eventually became nominally Christian. The second began by being Christian and ended by becoming largely secularized.

There is no doubt that we have now emerged from this last period, when the idea of subordination *for the sake of mission* was somewhat unfamiliar and uncongenial. Now, in many places, the situation of the Church bears more resemblance to that which we find in the New Testament, and it is there that we also find an emphasis on subordination.

By subordination we are not implying that mission as an activity is subordinate to other Christian activities. It is always primary, not secondary. We are implying that the living

[1] See M. A. C. Warren, *Caesar the Beloved Enemy*, SCM Press 1955, especially chapter 1.

agents of mission must normally accept the principle of subordination if the mission is to be rightly discharged.

First there is subordination to the powers that be.

> Let every person be subject to the governing authorities. For there is no authority except from God, and those that exist have been instituted by God (Rom. 13.1 RSV).

> Be subject for the Lord's sake to every human institution, whether it be to the emperor as supreme, or to governors as sent by him . . . (I Pet. 2.13, 14 RSV).

> Remind them to be submissive to rulers and authorities, to be obedient . . . (Tit. 3.1 RSV).

All these words were addressed to Christians in a missionary situation, often living in a hostile atmosphere. In some communist countries today the Church is taking these admonitions seriously and rediscovering their real relevance. Prophetic Christian voices are saying that the Church must not 'develop into an underground movement if it does not want to forfeit the promise given to it', because 'our state (East Germany) is an authority in the sense of Romans 13'. This is the context in which at least one Church is confessing that it has not loved enough. 'This is the only thing we have in our power to give to the state—a word of love from the God of love.'[1] If this is valid in a Marxist country, it is equally valid in a Muslim or Buddhist country. It is as much outside the proper sphere of the Christian mission to be anti-government as it is to seek government favours. Jesus was neither a Zealot seeking the overthrow of Roman rule nor a Sadducee taking dubious advantage of it. This is not to say that there are not times when *the indigenous Church* of a particular country must *in its prophetic ministry* address the Word of God to the state and its government. But that is a ministry quite distinct from its missionary activity, and it will not be an occasion for asking favours. All engaged in mission, whether nationals or foreigners, must accept subordination to the powers that be,

[1] *Pro-Existence: Christian Voices in East Germany*, ed. Elisabeth Adler, SCM Press 1964, 42, 40, 44.

friendly, neutral, or hostile, though subordination is not acquiescence. In the future the best the Church may hope for is to be allowed to continue its mission in purely secularized states, but it is improbable that this will often be the case.

Those who have studied their Bible and their history will not be alarmed unduly, if they will meditate on God's providential raising up and casting down of states and empires. Without a doctrine of Providence mission would be not merely disheartening but almost impossible; with it the ethics of subordination can be accepted as both logical and best.

Subordination, however, extends beyond the Christian attitude to the State. There is also a subordination to ways of thought and behaviour, to circumstances and susceptibilities, to the situations of those among whom the agents of the mission live and work. St Paul regarded this as a vital principle of mission.

> I am a free man and own no master; but I have made myself every man's servant, to win over as many as possible. To Jews I became like a Jew, to win Jews; as they are subject to the Law of Moses, I put myself under that law to win them although I am not myself subject to it. To win Gentiles, who are outside the law, I made myself like one of them, although I am not in truth outside God's law, being under the law of Christ. To the weak I became weak, to win the weak. Indeed, I have become everything in turn to men of every sort, so that in one way or another I may save some. All this I do for the sake of the Gospel, to bear my part in proclaiming it (I Cor. 9.19-23).

Here subordination is applied in an unmistakably missionary context; it is part of Paul's missionary methodology. It involves imagination, flexibility, adaptability, characteristics which have marked a few of the great missionary pioneers but have more often been neglected by the rank and file. Evidently Paul starts with the assumption that as a missionary he must be accepted in any community which he would win. But to belong to a group means to subordinate oneself to it—this is the condition of acceptability. The crucial importance of belonging has not always been fully recognized by those con-

cerned with the Christian mission. Although the first agents
of mission will usually come from outside any community—
though not invariably—they can be effective only as they
work and witness from within. They cannot remain outsiders
and achieve very much. The concept of 'belonging' is of much
greater significance than that of 'identification'. The dictionary
defines 'identity' as 'absolute sameness'. If words are to retain
their true meaning this is obviously impossible for any individual to attain in relation to another, notwithstanding the
question of a different race and culture. And identification
has often been interpreted somewhat superficially as 'going
native', wearing the clothes, eating the food, of Asians and
Africans. This is not what most of them want or expect from
missionaries, any more than the best missionaries wish to
westernize them. None can lose their identity or shake off
their past, and to try to do so often results in something little
better than a charade. The missionary is valued just because
he is different; this is a major part of his significance. But to
belong and to be seen and felt to belong is a very different
thing. This is greatly desired and immensely appreciated when
it happens. Here is the theological reason for a long spell of
service rather than a short one, which seems little more than
an excursion to those at the other end of the line. Such belonging requires a willingness to be subject. Mission means
subordination.

The practical outworking of this attitude will vary with time
and place. Indications of what it may mean can be seen in St
Paul's words quoted above, particularly if we substitute
modern parallels. To the Muslims the servant of the Gospel
must become like a Muslim and do his utmost to be acceptable to them to the point of belonging; to the beat groups he
becomes 'as one of them'; to the humanist, to the rebel, to the
existentialist, and the rest. But mission is not a fifth column
activity.

> We have renounced disgraceful, underhanded ways; we refuse
> to practise cunning or to tamper with God's word, but by the
> open statement of the truth we would commend ourselves to
> every man's conscience (II Cor. 4.2 RSV).

There can be no Trojan Horse methods, nothing comparable to the deceptive type of infiltration which is part of the communist programme. Wherever missionaries have engaged in this kind of thing, the results have been disastrous and years of patient work by other Christians in building up trust have been destroyed overnight. The infiltrator, of course, always remains an outsider, at least inwardly and beneath his disguise. But the true agent of the Christian mission belongs inwardly, even though he may look very different outwardly. He is one with those whom he has chosen to serve; he subordinates himself to the structures, the manners, and the thought-patterns of their society; he accommodates himself, as Paul recommends, to the utmost, but always 'under the law of Christ' which alone sets him his bounds.

This concept of subordination arises directly out of the Lordship of Jesus Christ. If Jesus is Lord, all who acknowledge him are his servants. The central Christian affirmation implies therefore the servanthood of the Church. This is the theological origin of the doctrine of subordination with its immense consequences for the Christian mission. St Paul resorts to extravagant language to emphasize his subordination to Christ. He is his bond-slave, his underling. Having found his spiritual freedom by accepting this spiritual bondage, he then renounces his freedom and enters into another kind of bondage in order to 'win' (the word is Paul's) men for Jesus Christ. 'Though I am free from all men, I have made myself a slave to all, that I might win the more' (I Cor. 9.19 RSV). There is no other way of entry into the tightly-knit groupings of men and their infinite variety. And, as we shall see in the next section, unless the servant of Christ can enter a particular society or group and be accepted and allowed to belong, all attempts at mission are vain.

Not all service is mission; not all service need be Christian. Some of the new religions of Japan (e.g. Tenrikyo and Ittoen) have a profound sense of service. And with Christianity itself there is a place for distinterested service which has nothing to do with mission. It is not the less Christian for that, but its motive and purpose may be quite different. Nevertheless, all

mission must be service, in some sense of that word. Mission
cannot be undertaken anywhere except in servant form.
Christians concerned with mission must be ready to function
as the servants of God to humanity. In the long run it is the
character of the servant rather than the nature of the service
which counts—the singer, not the song. The service itself may
not be mission; but the pre-condition of mission is always a
willingness to be a servant, especially in the sphere of human
relationships. And in the last analysis the need to be a slave
to all, which Paul accepted, is but a re-statement of the Gospel
ethic (see Mark 10.43-45; Luke 22.25-27). Christian subordination is a mutual rather than a hierarchical concept : 'Be subject to one another out of reverence for Christ' (Eph. 5.21).
'Through love be servants of one another' (Gal. 5.13 RSV).
'Rivalry and personal vanity should have no place among you,
but you should humbly reckon others better than yourselves.
You must look to each other's interest and not merely to your
own' (Phil. 2.3, 4). There can be no mission without subordination. Undoubtedly this is the hardest thing about mission
today, both for the national and the foreign missionary. It is
a concept which goes right back behind all our imperialisms
and the Christendom which Constantine inaugurated to the
Church of the first three centuries. If the members of younger
churches and the missionaries serving them both practised
the ethic of subordination, some of the worst tensions would
be resolved and a new chapter could start.

MISSION AS PENETRATION

Jesus used two vivid metaphors to describe the relation of
his Church to the world : light and salt. What they have in
common is their capacity to penetrate and at the same time
to remain distinct (Matt. 5.13-16). Light stands over against
darkness, distinct from it but penetrating it. 'The light shines
in the darkness, and the darkness has not overcome it' (John
1.5 RSV). Salt is inserted into food, but it retains its distinctive
flavour and preserves the food from decay. It goes right in but
remains itself. These figures of speech envisage the Church

engaging with the world, entering into relationships, thrusting itself into the secular, yet remaining itself. There can be no mission without penetration.

It is important to give full weight to the strength of the Lord's words. He does not say that Christians are to be *like* light and *like* salt. He says: 'You *are* salt to the world. . . . You *are* light to the world.' And although he was speaking to a relatively small group of people, none of them very significant, he sees their commitment to him as having *cosmic* effects. To be a Christian is not merely to add a little more light to one's village or neighbourhood, but to the world! Moreover, his concern is not that they should become something which they are not already, but that being what they are—salt and light —they should not lose their character or allow their function to be misappropriated.

> If salt becomes tasteless, how is its saltness to be restored? It is now good for nothing but to be thrown away and trodden under foot. . . . When a lamp is lit, it is not put under the meal-tub, but on the lamp-stand, where it gives light to everyone in the house.

In other words, what they are already as Christians has immediate and inevitable implications for the world. They are to affect the world in a way analogous to that of light in darkness and salt in meant. Theirs is to be a penetrating presence. There is to be a quality about their life of which the world cannot remain unaware. St Paul used a similar image when he wrote:

> Thanks be to God, who in Christ always leads us in triumph, and through us spreads the fragrance of the knowledge of him everywhere. For we are the aroma of Christ to God among those who are being saved and among those who are perishing (II Cor. 2.14, 15 RSV).

That which gives off a pleasant aroma is something of which others cannot but be aware. Perfume penetrates. The Church's

mission in the world—and Paul was writing here primarily of
missionary activity—was to be like the releasing of fragrance
which would carry the knowledge of Christ everywhere.

It is worth noting in passing that of these three images salt
and incense have sacrificial associations. There is not much
chance of the Christian community penetrating society without some kind of sacrifice. 'With all your offerings you shall
offer salt,' said the Levitical law (Lev. 2.13), as every Jew
would know, and incense was itself a sacrificial offering (e.g.
Ex. 30.1-8; Isa. 60.6, etc.). We should also note that the effects
of light, salt, and perfume are out of all proportion to their size
or quantity. The light from one candle can banish darkness
from a large room; a pinch of salt can flavour a whole meal; a
drop of perfume can pervade all one's clothes. The influence
of the Church was to depend on its quality not on its size. The
Church does not need to be large before it can engage in
mission or begin to have a missionary effect on the surrounding situation.

The Church's calling to be a penetrating force in its relation
to the world involves it in a delicate paradox of existence. It
has not always kept the balance and in its history it has veered
unevenly between two extremes. Either it has been so worldly
itself, so secularized, that as an institution it has been virtually
indistinguishable from secular institutions; or it has been so
unworldly and remote from the secular as to have neither
contact with it nor influence on it. At both extremes mission
becomes impossible : at the one because the Church is too
much identified with the secular, at the other because it is not
in the secular at all. Wherever the Church falls into either of
these positions, it ceases to be the light of the world and the
salt of the earth. So far as I know it was A. R. Vidler who
coined the phrase 'holy worldliness'.[1] There could hardly be
a better definition of this paradoxical relation. For the Church
is called to be holy and worldly at the same time, and it is by
being both together that its penetrating mission becomes possible. Being thoroughly in the world, sharing in the world's
agonies, glad of the world's progress and delights, will keep

[1] See A. R. Vidler, *Essays in Liberality*, SCM Press 1957, 95ff.

the Church worldly in the proper sense. Being 'children of light', 'salty Christians', will keep the Church holy in the proper sense.

Something of the effect of the Christian community upon its environment is envisaged by St Paul.

> Though you were once all darkness, now as Christians you are light. Live like men who are at home in daylight, for where light is, there all goodness springs up, all justice and truth. Make sure what would have the Lord's approval; take no part in the barren deeds of darkness, but show them up for what they are (Eph. 5.7-11).

The Church, it appears, is meant to have both cathartic and catalytic effects, and this can happen only by real Christian penetration. Catalysis is defined by the dictionary as the 'effect produced by a substance that without undergoing change itself aids chemical change in other bodies'. Is not this precisely the function of the Body of Christ in relation to the body politic? The Church is in the world in order that the world may eventually be changed because of its presence and its witness.

In the West today we are not living at a time when Christians can be charged with being too distinct from the world, even though the Church as a worshipping community often gives the impression of a worship having little bearing on the surrounding life. But most Christians are far less vividly distinct from their non-Christian neighbours than would be the case in at least some of the younger churches where Christianity is still fairly new. The Church in the West seems to be in a phase when it is very concerned to be 'identified' with the world and in danger of forgetting its calling to be distinct and holy.

> The 'Western world' lives and lets live. The effect of this seemingly ideal condition is that this Western world is, in fact . . . the most dangerous spot for the Church to live in. The most dangerous, because it is constantly tempted to function as an ingredient and not as the salt of the world.[1]

[1] H. Kraemer, *A Theology of the Laity*, Lutterworth 1958, 112.

A good deal of scorn has been poured on the more unworldly
movements marking other periods of Christian history—
monasticism, puritanism, pietism. We need to do more than
find scapegoats and give them labels; it is nothing like so
simple as this. But our danger is the reverse of theirs. The
insidious temptations to compromise or syncretism are as
strong as ever in the West and in the younger churches. When
this happens mission ends, for penetration has been succeeded
by absorption.

What are the ways of penetration? Three examples may be
given. First, letting the laity be the Church. Clericalism in any
form is the chief enemy of Christian expansion and mission
by penetration. The Church is to encounter the world primarily
through its laity, not through its clergy.

> For years talking about the laity has meant talking about their
> place in the Church gathered for worship, instruction and govern-
> ment; now it means talking about their calling to be the Church
> in the world. At last the fact that the layman spends the main
> part of his time in industry or commerce or television is being
> treated as something more than incidental.[1]

D. T. Niles has urged the need to understand the ordained
ministry as something provided to maintain the lay character
of the Christian community.

> From this arises the hope of so de-professionalizing the
> ordained ministry by disentangling the threefold functions of
> prophet, priest, and pastor, that these functions will not neces-
> sarily be bound up together in one person, but will be seen as
> the functions of the Church which the Church fulfils through
> different persons and in several ways.[2]

Where the laity are given their chance and where they take
it, things begin to happen. Stewardship campaigns have been a
case in point. Basil Moss has described how the layman is
beginning to discover the full reach of his own vocation and
ministry in the world.

[1] Kathleen Bliss, *We the People*, SCM Press 1963, 29.
[2] D. T. Niles, *Upon the Earth*, Lutterworth Press 1962, 174.

His new self-awareness as a Christian frontiersman leads him to demand more training, more support, more help than ever before. He requires from his parish priest, greater love, better theology, more holiness. If he expresses sharper criticism of the autocratic or incompetent exercise of clerical authority, who shall blame him? The reorientation of the Church towards the world necessarily involves reorientation of the clergy towards the committed laity and vice versa. They are colleagues in mission and ministry.[1]

And it goes without saying that if the clergy are effectively to teach the laity they must be equally ready to let the laity teach them. There are very few congregations anywhere in the world today where some, if not many, laymen do not possess much higher educational attainments and a much wider experience of life than their minister. If the Christian community in any place is to penetrate its surrounding society in terms of mission, this can only come about by a truly mutual partnership between clergy and laity. Kraemer has said that the Church is called to be an interfering community,[2] but if it is to interfere effectively it must know what it is doing and act responsibly.

A second way of penetration is by living on the frontier. It is true that in one sense of the word all laymen are frontiersmen, and this expression has just been used above. Every day they are crossing frontiers of all kinds in their work and so have opportunities for witness rarely, if ever, afforded to the clergy. But there are some frontiers which are stubbornly closed to all Christian influence, and certain people have a special calling to try to penetrate these. Usually they require specialists of some kind rather than amateurs, and much patience. Islam presents one such frontier. Industry is another. Some intellectual circles in universities and institutes of technology have closed their doors to Jesus Christ and his representatives. The worker-priest experiment in France was an attempt to penetrate one such frontier. One of these priests describes how the experience of living as and with the working-class changed them because there was a mutual penetration.

[1] Basil S. Moss, *Clergy Training Today*, SPCK 1964, 19.
[2] Op. cit., 185.

So we changed: we were not only soldiers fighting for a cause, we were being transformed in their being, in the very name of the mission. . . . We were rejected, as the working class is rejected by the established order, on account of our active participation in the labour struggle, and because the Church, through the majority of her members and institutions, defends a régime against which we fight alongside the working class with all our might because it is oppressive and unjust.[1]

We need not be side-tracked by the controversial elements in this quotation, which is in any case describing an extreme type of penetration. What is significant is the experience of being transformed as they penetrated the frontier. Some will no doubt say that this was tantamount to the salt losing its savour. This really misses the point, which is that they themselves were changed, not their faith or the Gospel they were presenting. We may also notice that it is all of a piece with what was said in our section on subordination about the need for belonging and its consequences, in this case painful ones. And it is all of a piece with the dilemma of the missionary, which we were considering earlier still, and with the cross of his rejection which will occupy our attention in a later chapter. Penetration has its dangers.

There are plenty of other frontiers where those on the adventure of the Christian mission will not make any dent until they have met with a lot of danger.

A third type of penetration is that undertaken by the missionary, the man or woman, trained and dedicated, who is sent by one Church as its gift to another Church. The missionary goes in order to give himself completely to another Church, another land, another people. In the spirit of Abraham the missionary answers that call of God which says, 'Go from your country to the land that I will show you'. His commitment is like that of Ruth's—'your people shall be my people'. His calling is to belong to them, to be one of them, to penetrate, so far as he may, in love and understanding, to the heart and thinking of another people. 'It is our life-task to make bridges

[1] Quoted in *Priests and Workers*, ed. David L. Edwards, SCM Press 1961, 50f.

into (men's) minds.'[1] John the Baptist described himself as a roadmaker, preparing a path for the Lord in that most unpromising place, the wilderness, where roads are not expected and travel is not encouraged. But the road which the prophet builds, a road of understanding, is to be both the way down which the Lord comes, revealing his glory, and the way by which his redeemed people go out of captivity into freedom (Isa. 40.3-5, 9-11; John 1.23).

The preposition which goes with penetration is 'into'. There are two great texts in the New Testament which provide a further clue to its meaning. The first is that command with which the Gospel ends. 'Go into all the world' (Mark 16.15). Nothing is to be immune from Christian penetration. Mission is to touch every aspect and area of the whole world's life. The second is a word about the nature and cost of penetration. 'Unless a grain of wheat falls into the earth and dies, it remains alone; but if it dies, it bears much fruit' (John 12.24). P. T. Forsyth preached a remarkable sermon on this text entitled 'The Fatherhood of Death'.[2] There is no fruitful penetration in the realm of the spirit without sacrifice. Mission accepts this as its condition, knowing all the time —to quote Forsyth's great sermon—that 'the missionary history of the Church is Christ's slow entrance on the right which he set up once for all in his Cross'. This final penetration of the world by Christ its Lord is the fulfilment of that which began when he first sent his disciples 'on ahead of him, two by two, into every town and place where he himself was about to come' (Luke 10.1).

'Whenever and wherever I see a missionary,' wrote D. T. Niles, 'I am aware that I am seeing a person who is away from home because of the Gospel of Jesus Christ. . . . The missionary is the result of the continuing explosion of the Gospel.'[3]

MISSION AS MEDIATION

'There is one God, and also one mediator between God and men, Christ Jesus, himself man' (I Tim. 2.5). Nothing that

[1] Kenneth Cragg, *The Call of the Minaret*, Oxford 1956, 274.
[2] See his *Missions in Church and State*, chapter I.
[3] *Upon the Earth*, 170.

follows in this section will forget this or be intended to weaken
its force as a theological statement. But in its context it is not
suggesting that there are no other processes of mediation or no
other middle-men; it is claiming that Jesus Christ is the only
mediator of divine salvation, for he 'sacrificed himself to win
freedom for all mankind'. He is the one mediator of salvation.
Nevertheless, the Gospel of this salvation has to be mediated to
men, and those who give themselves to the mission of the
Gospel are to that extent exercising a ministry of mediation. It
is important that this should be recognized as one more aspect
of mission.

The New Testament provides illustrations of this.

> One of the two who followed Jesus after hearing what John
> said was Andrew, Simon Peter's brother. The first thing he did
> was to find his brother Simon. He said to him, 'We have found
> the Messiah' (which is the Hebrew for 'Christ'). He brought Simon
> to Jesus . . . (John 1.40-42).

Andrew was being a mediator, as on two other occasions in
the Fourth Gospel, when he brought the boy with the loaves
and fishes to Jesus (6.8, 9) and when he brought the Greeks to
Jesus (12.21, 22). Introducing people to Jesus, now as then, is a
ministry of mediation. It is also called personal evangelism.

Again, at the feeding of the five thousand Jesus 'told the
people to sit down on the grass; then, taking the five loaves
and two fishes, he looked up to heaven, said the blessing, broke
the loaves, and gave them to the disciples; *and the disciples
gave them to the people*' (Matt. 14.19). Jesus was the mediator
of the miracle in that he did what was necessary; the disciples,
symbolizing the Church, had to mediate this to the multitude,
symbolizing the world. They could neither do what Jesus did
nor add to it. Their task was to make it available. This is a
ministry of mediation. In this sense all who minister the Word
and Sacraments, all who serve others in any way in the name
of Christ, are mediators.

Another example of this concept of mediation, so strongly
linked with mission, is the representative capacity in which
the servants of Jesus act.

To receive you is to receive me, and to receive me is to receive the One who sent me (Matt. 10.40).

Whoever listens to you listens to me; whoever rejects you rejects me. And whoever rejects me rejects the One who sent me (Luke 10.16).

In very truth I tell you, he who receives any messenger of mine receives me; receiving me, he receives the One who sent me (John 13.20).

In his exegesis of this saying in its Synoptic form T. W. Manson writes:

The messengers are, in a sense, the Kingdom of God itself. The solidarity is impressive. The disciple represents in the fullest sense Jesus, and Jesus represents in the fullest sense the Kingdom of God. What they offer is God's offer and what they claim is God's claim.[1]

Twice in St Paul's letters he refers to being received in this kind of way. The Galatians had received him 'as if I were an angel of God, as you might have welcomed Christ Jesus himself' (Gal. 4.14) when he first preached the Gospel to them, despite a physical ailment; and of the Thessalonians he could write: 'We thank God continually, because when we handed on God's message, you received it, not as the word of men, but as what it truly is, the very word of God at work in you who hold the faith' (I Thess. 2.13).

It is but a short step from this set of sayings to St Paul's extraordinarily bold claim, the shock of which has worn off through familiarity: 'We come therefore as Christ's ambassadors. It is as if God were appealing to you through us: in Christ's name, we implore you, be reconciled to God' (II Cor. 5.20). Here the language is strongly mediatorial: 'ambassadors', 'God appealing to you through us', 'in Christ's name'. The ambassador is a mediator in that he is related both to the one who sends him and to those to whom he is sent. It is the first whom he represents; it is the second whom he attempts to influence. The significance of the mediation theme is even

---

[1] T. W. Manson, *The Sayings of Jesus*, SCM Press 1949, 78.

C

stronger if we remember that Paul's claim about his ambassadorial role as a missionary is set within a passage about reconciliation. The deed of reconciliation is complete on God's side—it took place in the Cross of Jesus Christ. Now the knowledge of reconciliation and its acceptance on man's part has to be brought about. To this end 'he has enlisted us in this service of reconciliation' and 'he has entrusted us with the message of reconciliation' (vv. 18, 19). Just as Jesus once made possible a supply of food, but the food had to be distributed by the disciples; so the same Jesus made possible right relationship between God and man, but the deed and its effects have to be made known by his disciples. In both instances the disciples of Jesus are charged with a ministry of mediation *by the one mediator* between God and men! Mission is always mediation.

This is, of course, the principle of the Incarnation. In terms of mission there is a parallel between the relation of the Father to the Son and that of the Son to the Church. In order to make himself known to men God took a body, he became incarnate in his Son; he was mediated through the Son. His mission completed, the divine Son chose to make himself known to the world through his disciples; he was content to use them as his Body, to work through them. The Fourth Gospel is unambiguous about this. 'As the Father sent me, so I send you' (John 20.21): and in the great prayer: 'As thou hast sent me into the world, I have sent them into the world' (17.18). The mission is one throughout, but with the resurrection of Jesus it enters a new, a secondary, phase. When God acted and spoke through his Son, he had a perfect image and instrument, and there was no distortion. With the Church, made up of sinners, this cannot be so. But the pattern of the mission is the same and it works on the same incarnational principle. The imperfections of the Church and its disobedience are indeed daunting factors, but as Bishop Stephen Neill has reminded us:

> If we are concerned about the work of God, we had better lose no time in coming to terms with the instrument, because there is no other; and what God is prepared to acknowledge as his own, it ill becomes us to despise.[1]

[1] S. C. Neill, *The Unfinished Task*, Edinburgh House 1957, 34.

In the first phase Jesus was the missionary. In the second phase the Church is 'the corporate missionary of the Gospel to the world'.[1] The second phase continues.

A major part of the problem of mission arises not out of the message but out of its mediators. How is the Church, as we know it, effectively to mediate the Gospel to the world? Is the greater stumbling-block the nature of the Gospel or the nature of the Church? Both present difficulties because in both God seems to have tied himself to the particular. Whatever faults may be found with the institutional Church—and there are plenty of people inside and outside who enjoy finding them—every Christian must allow one thing to the Church's credit. Apart from the Church none of us would *be* Christians. Each Christian is a Christian because Christ has been mediated to him through someone else, an Andrew to our Peter, probably through many agents and instruments and influences, all of which are the result of the Church. In so far as the Church is still making people Christian and keeping them Christian it is fulfilling its mission, at least in part.

But the Church's chief task in terms of mediation is to make Christianity visible, intelligible and desirable.[2] The hardest of these is to make it visible; for if it were more visible the other two would follow. It is easier to understand and to desire something seen than unseen. One of the earliest French worker-priests asked: 'Can our contemporaries truthfully say that they can *see any Christians*, any authentic Christians, as distinct from phantom Christians?'[3] In the Gospel, the Word of Christ, he wills to be audible; in the Church, the Body of Christ, he wills to be visible. In the preaching of the Word and in the life of the Church he is mediated, through human agents, and despite all the distortions due to sin and error, Christ submits to this and so makes himself still available in the world. The Church is called to make Christ so visible in its own life that the Gospel becomes intelligible and desirable.

[1] P. T. Forsyth, *Revelation Old and New*, Independent Press 1962, 34.
[2] I owe these three adjectives to Prof. H. A. Hodges in his *Christianity and the Modern World View*, SPCK 1962, 8.
[3] *Priests and Workers*, 69.

There is one other aspect of mediation as related to mission, which we should notice. It is a sense of vicarious liability. One instance of this occurs in Paul's letter to Philemon, in which he offers to take personal responsibility for Onesimus, the former runaway slave whom Paul had led to Christ.

> If, then, you count me partner in the faith, welcome him as you would welcome me. And if he has done you any wrong or is in your debt, put that down to my account (Philemon 18, 19).

We see here once again this solidarity of relationship in which Christians stand towards each other, evangelists and their converts being specially close. To take responsibility for another man's misdeeds, sometimes necessary in a truly priestly and pastoral ministry, is to exercise a ministry of mediation. But the most important part of this is seen in intercession, the kind of mediatorial prayer whose strength is derived from the solidarity that exists between the one who prays and those for whom he prays. Moses was a mediator in this sense when Israel, God's youthful people, had sinned by reverting to idolatry. 'Therefore he said he would destroy them—had not Moses, his chosen one, stood in the breach before him' (Ps. 106.23 RSV). In the Exodus account Moses prays: 'Alas, this people have sinned a great sin. . . . But now, if thou wilt forgive their sin—and if not, blot me, I pray thee, out of thy book which thou hast written' (Ex. 32.32). St Paul reached the same pitch of solidarity-feeling toward the Jews who had rejected Christ. 'In my heart there is great grief and unceasing sorrow. For I could even pray to be outcast from Christ myself for the sake of my brothers, my natural kins-folk' (Rom. 9.2, 3). This is a missionary praying. George Whit-field (1714-70), in a sermon summoning men to repent, said: 'Believe me, I am willing to go to prison or death for you, but I am not willing to go to heaven without you.'

This spirit is produced as mission takes the form of media-tion. If mission is to have any reach about it, the agents of mission must feel something of this solidarity with those to whom they are sent as ambassadors. Towards them they will do their utmost to commend the Christian message by being themselves acceptable : 'by the open statement of the truth we would commend ourselves to every man's conscience in the sight of God' (II Cor. 4.2 RSV). And towards God those who are his ambassadors to men become in turn intercessors on men's behalf. The downward traffic of grace and the upward traffic of prayer create a road upon which God and men may meet.

MISSION AS INTEGRATION

The choice for this heading had to be made from a number of words whose shades of meaning differ only slightly, such as unification or incorporation, or even reconciliation or transformation. That which we are seeking to describe is the ultimate aim of mission, what it is meant to achieve in men, in history, in society. The dominant idea in the New Testament is of a drawing together of men into a unity unknown outside Christ, and each of these words suggests some aspects of this unity. We have chosen integration because it is the shortest and least technical.

Two strands run through the Bible : we may call them the Adam-and-Eve strand and the Cain-and-Abel strand. The first represents the original and intended unity of mankind, the second the divisions that appear within that unity and rend it. Both are there from the beginning and both are at work all through. For the Bible shows in picture form and history the destructive forces which divide and the unifying forces which unite. Cain and Abel, like Jacob and Esau, David and Absalom, and the disciples of the Lord, quarrel : this is the story of man from the start and of the Church from the start. But at the same time there are redemptive and unifying movements : God calls Abraham and creates Israel to be an integrating factor in whom all the families of the earth should be blessed. Jesus creates and commissions the Church that it should make disciples of all nations and that they should be baptized into the name of the Father, the Son, and the Holy Spirit, and so participate in the oneness of the life of God himself.

There is, however, not merely a parallelism between the

destructive and the integrating forces; the unifying powers are themselves divisive before they move towards union. Possibly one reason for this is that the potency of any force for unity will depend to a great extent on its being a concentrated unity in itself. The unity will of course be enriched and strengthened by diversity, but it may be weakened by too great a diffuseness. So the seed of Israel passes through Isaac but not Ishmael, through Jacob but not Esau. Only in the fourth generation do all the sons partake of the promise and embody, outwardly at any rate, Israel's unity. Man's unity in Adam is necessarily diffuse and infinitely variegated. The unity of the people of God in Israel is much more concentrated and specific, and this is brought about by the lopping off process which we have just noted. The same thought occurs repeatedly in the prophet Jeremiah, to whom the Lord said : 'See, I have set you this day over nations and over kingdoms, to pluck up and to break down, to destroy and to overthrow, to build and to plant' (Jer. 1.10; cf. 18.7; 31.28; 45.4). Before there can be integration there must be a preliminary disintegration. That unity which is the purpose of God for his people has to be purged from impurities and falsehoods and all that defiles (Rev. 21.27; 22.15; cf. Isa. 52.1).

Jesus said some uncomfortable words along these lines, teaching that the smaller unities would have to be destroyed before the greater unity could be realized.

> Do you suppose I came to establish peace on earth? No indeed, I have come to bring division. For from now on, five members of a family will be divided, three against two and two against three; father against son and son against father, mother against daughter and daughter against mother, mother against son's wife and son's wife against her mother-in-law (Luke 12.51-53; Matt. 10.35, 36).

These smaller, traditional unities themselves create and perpetuate division, and we see this in slavery, tribalism, the caste system, feudalism, nationalism, racialism, as one human block organizes itself against another or against the rest. Because some will always prefer the *status quo* to what is new, even families are divided through incompatible allegiances. And the most divisive thing of all is allegiance to Jesus Christ himself, for 'he who is not with me is against me' (Matt. 12.30). It is therefore on the other side of commitment to Jesus Christ that the greater integration is possible, as the old allegiances and their solidarities give way to a new life, a new creation, in whose staggeringly diverse unity all lesser unities lose their selfish meanings and their demonic power.

The richness of the new unity in Christ was a source of constant wonder and delight to St Paul. So he describes that integration which is the aim of all mission in classic words :

> Through faith you are all sons of God in union with Christ Jesus. Baptized into union with him, you have all put on Christ as a garment. There is no such thing as Jew and Greek, slave and freeman, male and female; for you are all one person in Jesus Christ. But if you thus belong to Christ, you are the 'issue' of Abraham and so heirs by promise (Gal. 3.26-29).

> You have discarded the old nature with its deeds and have put on the new nature, which is being constantly renewed in the image of its Creator and brought to know God. There is no question here of Greek and Jew, circumcised and uncircumcised, barbarian, Scythian, freeman, slave; but Christ is all, and is in all (Col. 3.9-11).

Something of the startling relevance of the Christian mission to the contemporary world might become apparent if it were more often presented in terms of its final aim—the integration of mankind, the reverse of the Fall, as the Day of Pentecost was the reverse of Babel. The inadequacies and the pain of the lesser unities are obvious enough, even when they try to enlarge their borders. The unity of nearly every African country is threatened by tribalism. The Pan-Africanism, which is the dream of Africa's most far-seeing statesmen, is threatened by nationalism. The unity of countries like India and Ceylon is threatened by the divisions of language. Arab unity, so obvious a thing by virtue of a common language and a common religion, is threatened by Arab nationalisms. The unity of the United States and of South Africa is threatened by racialism. The unity of the United Nations is threatened by ideologies. Even the Communist world is itself bitterly divided from within. Theologically none of these unities is adequate because none of them is able to deal with the problem of human sin, the root cause of all division and destructiveness. They are unities based on things that men hold in common, not on a redeemed relationship with God.

This is the point at which the Christian message cuts across all other patterns of human unity and offers something more deeply based because it centres in God and not in man. In the process of doing this even the old unities can break up, but this is precisely what Jesus said would happen in the accomplishment of his mission which is also ours. The Church, therefore, must accept some responsibility for bringing disintegration into many different societies of the world, especially Africa, though secular forces have also played their part. Something of the pain this has caused can be felt by reading African poetry and African novels. Two, whose very titles suggest this, are *Things Fall Apart* and *No Longer at Ease* by the Nigerian, Chinua Achebe. But it is the same story fundamentally in the modern West, as our own poets and novelists faithfully depict, and a German sociologist has written of 'the Broken West'.[1] The process of disintegration is repetitive and will continue to be until the one true reconciliation is found and entered into. It is of this that St Paul writes when, in the same passage as he speaks about the new creation, the new world, the new being, he declares: 'God was in Christ reconciling the world to himself, no longer holding men's misdeeds against them. . . . Christ was innocent of sin, and yet for our sake God made him one with the sinfulness of men, so that in him we might be made one with the goodness of God himself' (II Cor. 5.17, 19, 21). Being 'made one with the goodness of God himself' *is* integration, and within this oneness is the final pattern of unity towards which the whole Christian mission strives.

The New Testament throughout is clear that this exists only

[1] See essay by Marlies Cremer in *The Missionary Church in East and West*, ed. C. C. West and D. M. Paton, SCM Press 1959.

in Christ. The Christ who divides the world, because in his
ministry his word is a sharp two-edged sword, unites it ultimately by means of his death.

> Caiaphas, who was High Priest that year, said, 'You know
> nothing whatever; you do not use your judgment; it is more to
> your interest that one man should die for the people, than that
> the whole nation should be destroyed.' He did not say this of
> his own accord, but as the High Priest in office that year, he was
> prophesying that Jesus would die for the nation—die not for the
> nation alone but to gather together the scattered children of
> God. So from that day on they plotted his death (John 11.50-53).

It was shortly after this that Jesus said, 'Now is the hour of
judgment for this world; now shall the Prince of this world be
driven out. And I shall draw all men to myself, when I am
lifted up from the earth' (John 12.31, 32). Drawing all men to
himself is the object of the mission of Jesus and his Church.
But John deliberately leaves the meaning of 'lifted up' am-
biguous, because, as with so many of his expressions, he wishes
to convey two meanings simultaneously. The lifting up was
the lifting up on the Cross, just as the brazen serpent was
lifted up in the wilderness that men might be healed (John
3.14). It was also his ascent into glory. Man does the first—his
execution and condemnation. God does the second—his exalta-
tion and vindication. So it is Jesus, crucified and risen, who
alone draws 'all men', and he draws them to himself. He is the
integrator, the one creator and centre of unity for the whole
race.

There is neither need nor space to examine all the other New
Testament images which convey this same Christian conviction. An obvious one is the new Adam (Rom. 5.12-17; I Cor.
15.22); another is St Paul's favourite phrase 'in Christ'. The
heart of Paul's religion is to be united with Christ. For this
reason the two great sacraments of the Gospel are an integral
part of the Christian mission, for it is by Holy Baptism that
men come to be 'in Christ'; and it is by the Eucharist that they
are given grace to remain 'in Christ'—'very members incor-
porate' in his mystical body. Any missionary enterprise which

is essentially non-sacramental, whether in theology or practice, is omitting something which was central to the apostolic mission of the early Church and losing sight of that great goal which Paul describes as growing up into Christ.

> He is the head, and on him the whole body depends. Bonded and knit together by every constituent joint, the whole frame grows through the due activity of each part, and builds itself up in love (Eph. 4.16).

Quite deliberately we are not discussing the unity of the Church in this section, though of course it belongs here. There is however a vast literature on the theology of unity, but there is relatively little on the theology of mission, which is the theme of this book. It is generally admitted that mission and unity hang together and the point need no longer be argued. But the strands are not always uncomplicated. Unity is the end of mission; yet mission is the means to unity. Jesus prays that his disciples may all be one that the world may believe (John 17.21-23), but from the beginning the Gospel has been preached by those who were not at one (Phil. 1.15-18), and although St Paul is distressed by this he does not regard it as an unmitigated disaster. 'What does it matter? One way or another, in pretence or in sincerity, Christ is set forth, and for that I rejoice.' It may be ironical but it is surely true that more has been achieved in history by divided churches preaching the Gospel than by great monolithic churches failing to do so. It is more important to see unity in the context of mission than mission in the context of unity. Until now the greatest step forward in Christian reunion was that taken in 1947 which led to the inauguration of the Church of South India. It happened there because all the negotiators and church leaders were primarily concerned with winning the millions of India for Jesus Christ. They sought unity not in a narrow ecclesiastical sense but as part of their missionary obedience. And what they sought for the right reason they found. It is questionable whether real progress towards Christian unity and integration will be made elsewhere until there has been a recovery of this sense of mission to the world.

MISSION AS CONSUMMATION

Mission began with God and ends with God—like creation. We are caught up into it, but neither the beginning nor the end are in our hands or within our sight. Nevertheless, it does end. There is to be a climax, a consummation, when across the world and history and the Church the words 'mission accomplished' will in effect be written. The Bible never loses sight of the end, however distant. It is described in various images. 'The earth shall be full of the knowledge of the Lord as the waters cover the sea' (Isa. 11.9; Hab. 2.14). 'All the ends of the earth shall see the salvation of our God' (Isa. 52.10). 'All flesh shall come and worship before me' (Isa. 66.23). In the New Testament there are the parables of the Kingdom with their sense of time running towards an end, when decisions are made, the day of opportunity closes, judgment operates, and the day of destiny dawns. There are also the visions of the Apocalypse in which the kingdom of this world becomes the Kingdom 'of our Lord and his Christ' and he shall reign for ever and ever (Rev. 11.15), and the kings of the earth bring their glory into the city of God (Rev. 21.22-26). All this suggests that mission eventually ends and its purpose is completed.

But what sort of an end is it to be? We cannot embark on a full-scale discussion of the Last Things, but it is important to notice that there is some relation between the fulfilment of the Church's mission and the end. 'This gospel of the Kingdom will be proclaimed throughout the earth as a testimony to many nations; and then the end will come' (Matt. 24.14; cf. Mark 13.10). It is hard to be explicit about this relation of church history and world history and their bearing on each other. The Christian knows that they are both in God's hands, that they are related in a way that is largely hidden from our understanding now, and that they must both end in a final consummation. The Christian mission has something to contribute to that consummation of history in which it finds its own completion. Thus Oscar Cullmann has written:

The missionary proclamation of the Church, its preaching of

the gospel, gives to the period between Christ's resurrection and Parousia (coming) its meaning for redemptive history; and it has this meaning through its connection with Christ's present Lordship. . . . It is not the case that the coming of the Kingdom depends upon the success of this preaching; it depends rather upon the fact of the preaching.[1]

The question in many minds today is: Will the Christian mission be a success? Will all the effort and sacrifice have achieved anything worthwhile? It is a question that burns much more deeply in the Christian mind today than it did a hundred years ago when there was little doubt of the final issue. Let it be said at once that such Christian certainty as may be reached rests only on faith and not on calculation. But on this matter we may call in the help of three very different Christian thinkers. John Baillie writes:

> Our conclusion then is that the Christian faith does offer us a very confident hope for the future course of terrestrial history. It is a hope which has been too little represented in the Christian tradition, but to which we are now recalled. We must recover that sense of standing on the threshold of a new historical economy (or dispensation), that sense of a noble prospect opening out before us, that sense of the power of the Spirit and of the inexhaustible resources now available to us, that adventurous zeal for the renewal of humanity and that confidence in ultimate victory of which the New Testament is so full.[2]

Bishop Stephen Neill shares this hope, also held by John Macmurray and Oscar Cullmann:

> It seems clear that what the New Testament looks forward to is the triumph of God in time and within history, a triumph to be brought about solely by his own act, but at the same time dependent upon the preparatory work of the Church, without which God cannot move forward to the next step in the accomplishment of his great design.[3]

---

[1] O. Cullmann, *Christ and Time*, SCM Press 1951, 157, 160.
[2] John Baillie, *The Belief in Progress*, OUP 1950, 220.
[3] S. C. Neill, *The Unfinished Task*, Lutterworth 1957, 32.

The third writer we would cite is perhaps the most interesting, in that he is not writing about mission—Pierre Teilhard de Chardin. As a distinguished biologist and palaeontologist he delves far into the past and tries to look into the future. His view of the future is full of hope, for he sees the beginnings of new groupings, a new pattern of sociological unity deeper than anything we can imagine at present, which he calls the noosphere.

> Merely from looking at the external signs we can hardly fail to suspect that the great unrest which has pervaded our life in the West ever since the storm of the French Revolution springs from a nobler and deeper cause than the difficulties of a world seeking to recover some ancient equilibrium that it has lost. There is no question of shipwreck. What we are up against is the heavy swell of an unknown sea which we are just entering from behind the cape that protected us. . . . In these confused and restless zones in which present blends with future in a world of upheaval, we stand face to face with all the grandeur, the unprecedented grandeur, of the phenomenon of man.[1]

That is how de Chardin accounts for the present and looks expectantly to the more immediate future. But he also tries to peer into the distant scene and he speaks of 'the Omega Point'. On this all converges at the end of the world. For Christ, who is the principle of universal vitality, is to subdue everything under himself, to purify, to direct, and to superanimate.

> And when he has gathered everything together and transformed everything, he will close in upon himself and his conquests, thereby rejoining, in a final gesture, the divine focus he has never left.[2]

This is highly colourful language, which will attract some and dismay others, but it is only a reiteration of St Paul's doctrine, worked out so majestically in Ephesians 1, that in the

[1] Pierre Teilhard de Chardin, *The Phenomenon of Man*, Collins 1959, 214f.
[2] Ibid., 294.

fullness of time God will sum up or unite all things in Christ.
This is the ultimate goal and vision of the Christian mission.
This hope enables perseverance.

> What we are witnessing is the process by which more and
> more of the human race is being gathered up into that history
> whose centre is the cross and whose end is the final judgment
> and mercy of God. . . . World history is in the grip of Christ,
> is being propelled by him towards its ultimate issues, propelled
> through tribulation and conflict to a final consummation in
> which the judgment and mercy of God which are set forth in the
> Cross are finally and conclusively worked out.[1]

The consummation therefore implies a transformation.
Every creature, every power, will be subject to the Kingdom
and God will be all in all, 'everything to every one' (I Cor.
15.28). His love will have triumphed, pervading the universe,
and the final redemption, for which 'the whole created universe
groans in all its parts as if in the pangs of childbirth' (Rom.
8.22), will be a complete and eternal reality.

At the end of the last chapter we considered the problem of
failure and success which perplexes so many who look at the
Christian mission, whether from inside or outside. If, however,
we believe in God as the Creator of the world and the Lord of
history, and in Jesus Christ, the Alpha and the Omega, and
the supremacy of divine love, as revealed in him, we cannot
be in doubt about the final issue. At present we are like those
Galilean fishermen whose spokesman once said to Jesus,
'Master we toiled all night and caught nothing.' A little later
their mood was changed from bleak despair to overwhelming
wonder and gratitude as their nets were breaking with the
abundance of the catch. The story ends with a word from Jesus
which the early Church could not forget. 'From now on you
will be catching men' (Luke 5.1-11). This was to be the beginning of that mission whose end is to be the summing up of
all things in Christ. If words have any meaning the Lord is
assuring his Church that its labours and sufferings will not

[1] J. E. L. Newbigin in *The Missionary Church in East and West*, op.
cit., 82f.

ultimately be in vain. It was because the apostle Paul shared this conviction on the basis of faith in the resurrection, that he could write : 'work for the Lord always, work without limit, since you know that in the Lord your labour cannot be lost' (I Cor. 15.58). Those engaged in mission, however hard and unrewarding the toil, may continue undaunted, knowing that the end of mission is consummation, glory, joy unspeakable.

3

YOUNGER CHURCHES
A Way of Seeing

THE achievement of mission is to be seen in the life of the Church itself and especially of the churches in Africa, Asia and Latin America, whose existence is the result of the Christian mission in the last two centuries. There are many important reasons for studying these 'younger' churches. First, they are highly significant in themselves. Second, if relations between older and younger churches are to be good and fruitful they must be based on knowledge and understanding, not imagination and fancy. These relations may be subject to a good deal of strain in the next few years. And third, the younger churches furnish us with a laboratory in which we can gain fresh understanding of the Church in the New Testament, because in almost every respect they are so much closer to the New Testament than most of the western churches (outside the Iron Curtain). They provide us with vivid and living commentaries on the Acts of the Apostles and the letters of the apostles. I always feel nearer to the New Testament situation when I am in Africa or Asia than when I am in Europe or North America. It is quite possible to read through an epistle such as I Corinthians and find parallels or illustrations to every verse in these our sister churches. But there is one caution to remember in the study of churches. As fellow-Christians we cannot study a church as we might study fish in an aquarium, by detached observation. This is a dangerous pursuit and will not yield altogether accurate or helpful results. The best way to study a church is by active participation in its life, to be on the inside and not the outside.

The John who wrote the Revelation addressed it to seven

churches. In his book he included a letter to each of those
churches. There is reason to suppose that he regarded seven as
a symbolic number and that seven examples were sufficient
for his purpose. There is also reason to think that he chose
these particular seven because of the representative nature of
their problems. Martin Kiddle has argued that the letters form
a sevenfold discourse which is both an analysis of the whole
Church and a message to the whole Church. 'For John, Revelation was more than a diocesan charge; it was a prophetic
encyclical.'[1] At the time when John wrote they were all very
young churches, younger than some churches in Africa and
Asia today.

> Each of the seven letters contains an analysis of the life of
> the church addressed; its essential faults and virtues are singled
> out, and warning or praise accordingly allotted. Two of the
> churches, the first and the last, are threatened with complete
> extinction, since each lacks qualities essential to the profession
> of the Christian faith. Unqualified praise is given to the second
> and sixth churches. The three central churches are complimented
> and castigated in varying degrees, for in each of them there exists
> a mixture of good and bad elements; the faithful are promised
> rewards and the faithless are threatened with the severest punish-
> ments. The striking and deliberate symmetry of this design
> strengthens the conclusion which is to be drawn from the whole
> picture of the life of the seven churches. They are intended to
> epitomize Christian life throughout the world.[2]

No one can do for the Church of our day what John did for the
Church of his day, partly because the Church is so much
bigger, but also because no one has sufficient authority or
intimate knowledge. Nevertheless, without expounding the
letters in detail we may notice two points of deep theological
significance about John's way of looking at churches.

First, before John comes to describe his seven chosen cross-
sections of the Church through the ages and across the world,

[1] M. Kiddle, *Moffatt New Testament Commentary on the Revelation
of St John*, Hodder and Stoughton 1940, 18.
[2] Kiddle, op. cit., 6f.

he describes the Lord Christ in majesty. With a profound Christian instinct he does not dare to look at the Church until he has looked at Jesus Christ as he now is. The earthly prospect is seen in true Christian focus only after and in the light of the heavenly vision. Nor can there be any understanding of the Church if we look at it merely as a phenomenon, without having first worshipped the exalted Lord and come to realize something of his glory and might. For the nature and situation of the Church can be grasped only in so far as the nature and situation of Christ are recognized. No one therefore is at the right vantage point for seeing the Church until he has worshipped and adored the Christ. This should provide a clue to all our efforts at explaining or describing the Church. St Paul also had discovered that from within the New Being he could no longer look at anything 'from a human point of view' (II Cor. 5.16 RSV). We have things in the wrong order and the wrong perspective if we begin by looking at the Church and then turn to Christ. The prophet begins with Christ and then looks at the Church.

Secondly, John goes on to say three things about Christ and his relation to the Church. The churches are symbolized by seven golden lamp-stands and in their midst is one like a son of man (1.13f). Christ is in the midst of his churches wherever they may be. He is omnipresent to the Church. 'I am with you always, to the end of time' (Matt. 28.20; cf. John 14.23; Acts 18.10). John also likens the churches to stars and he sees these seven stars in Christ's right hand (1.16). Christ holds the Church in his hand. He is its ultimate protector and security. The Good Shepherd had once said of his sheep: 'I give them eternal life, and they shall never perish, and no one shall snatch them out of my hand' (John 10.28). He is omnipotent for his Church. The first letter begins by bringing both these concepts together again: 'These are the words of One who holds the seven stars in his right hand and walks among the seven lamps of gold' (2.1).

The third truth John sees about Christ and his Church is his omniscience of its life and affairs, of which he knows every secret and every detail. So each of the seven letters begins, after the introduction, with the words 'I know'. 'I know all your ways' (NEB). 'I know your works' (RSV). 'I know . . . your toil and your fortitude' (2.2). This word could still apply to most younger churches. 'I know how hard pressed you are, and poor—and yet you are rich; I know how you are slandered . . .' (2.9). This would still describe much of the Church in India and in the Muslim world. 'I know where you live; it is the place where Satan has his throne' (2.13)—a situation that still exists in many a village and many a town. 'I know all your ways, your love and faithfulness, your good service and your fortitude; and of late you have done even better than at first' (2.19). These words of encouragement are still spoken by the Lord to some of his churches. 'I know that though you have a name for being alive, you are dead' (3.2). There is more than one church of which this word is true today. 'I know all your ways; and look, I have set before you an open door, which no one can shut. Your strength, I know, is small, yet you have observed my commands and have not disowned my name' (3.8). Some weak churches are still facing open doors of great opportunity. 'I know you are neither hot nor cold' least in the West, but elsewhere too. Because Christ knows (3.15). Mediocrity is still the sin of much of the Church, not everything and yet still walks in the midst of his churches and holds them in his hands, we need not be afraid nor need we despair. There is no other *Christian* way of looking at churches.

We turn now to consider four particular aspects of younger churches which profoundly concern the Christian mission. They are: age, size, environment, security. In all these the younger churches are nearer than the western churches to the New Testament situation.

AGE

The churches in Africa and Asia *are* younger, whether they like it or not, though they certainly do not like being constantly reminded of the fact in a way that equates youth with inexperience. For this reason we are not encouraged to use the expression 'Younger Churches' today, but it is difficult to

know what to substitute for it, because the facts themselves do
not change.

It is certainly wrong to regard all young churches as infantile. It is equally wrong to regard all of them as wholly
adult, even though some of them have been hastened into
adulthood by circumstances, as for example in the Sudan. The
presence of too many missionaries, especially in positions of
power, may unnecessarily retard the adulthood of a church.
But even within adulthood, if we may pursue the human
analogy, there is a considerable difference between a youth of
18 who looks a man, and a man of 28, 48 and 78. The most
important elements of difference are due to experience and
outlook. Similarly, there is sure to be a considerable difference
between a church that is sixty years old, as in the Sudan, or
160 years old, as in India, or 1600 years old, as in Britain. The
difference is not that one is adult and another infantile, but
that one has had long experience and the other has had less.
Within adulthood itself there is a difference between older
and younger, each needing the other in a relation of interdependence. Youth sees visions, age dreams dreams. In youth
eyes are predominantly on the future; in age they are more
often on the past. Ideally and in its maturity the Church is
meant to have the best of both worlds, being old and young at
the same time, both in its membership, made up of individuals
of various ages, and in its family life, made up of churches of
various ages in partnership.

This idea is brought out picturesquely by St John, who
addresses the Christian community as children, fathers, and
young men (I John 2.12-14). Together as a community they are
meant to share the characteristics and experiences which
belong to the different age-groups. 'I write to you, my children,
because your sins have been forgiven for his sake.' The forgiveness of sins is the deep experience of a new-born church
as of a new-born Christian. 'I write to you, fathers, because
you know him who is from the beginning.' An ever deeper
knowledge of God through the years is the mark of the mature
Christian and the mature church. 'I write to you, young
men, because you have mastered the evil one.' The testing of

strength, the pursuit of victory, is the mark of youth which goes in for an athletic, militant, warrior attitude. And John repeats the three phrases. C. H. Dodd comments:

> The threefold arrangement is probably not much more than a rhetorical figure. All the privileges belong to all Christians, but emphasis and variety of expression are secured by distributing them into groups.[1]

Thus Christians have the innocence of childhood, the strength of youth, and the serene knowledge of age and experience. May we not see this as part of the richness of the Church also, and get beyond the making of the wrong kind of discrimination between older and younger churches?

It is important not to burke the facts about age, but neither must we give them too much weight. At the same time we do well to recognize that both old and young have their sensitivities. The young tend to be self-conscious and assertive. The old tend to be conservative and dislike being pushed about. This is true of churches and it is visibly true at many ecumenical or confessional congresses. We have to learn a *modus vivendi* within the one family. If the old are not to be sentimental and paternalistic and if the young are not to be intimidated and insincere, this is no easy matter. We may instance difficulties from each side. Younger churches wish to be treated as adult. They are entitled to this only in so far as they behave like adults, particularly in the business of taking criticism. At present it is almost impossible for anyone from an older church to make critical remarks about a church in Africa or Asia without being accused of imperialism or interference or worse. Younger churches are pathologically sensitive to the least word of disapproval. Yet their own criticisms of the older churches are unending. Many of these are entirely justified, but in adult relationships criticism must be mutual. This cannot be said to be the case today. On the other hand the older churches talk a good deal about reunion; they talk but do not act. The younger churches are understandably im-

[1] C. H. Dodd, *Moffatt Commentary on the Johannine Epistles*, Hodder and Stoughton 1946, 38.

patient with this and accuse the West of insincerity. When the
family life of a church is strong there can be constructive and
mutual criticism as one speaks the truth to another in love.
Where there is suspicion or resentment this is not possible. In
the Church of God relationships should be determined not by
age or seniority but by membership of the family. St Paul's
words about human relationships are equally relevant to
churches.

> Have done with spite and passion, all angry shouting and
> cursing, and bad feeling of every kind. Be generous to one
> another, tender-hearted, forgiving one another as God in Christ
> forgave you (Eph. 4.31, 32).

Churches have much forgiving to do, and some of this arises
from the strains of age-differences.

SIZE

Among human beings size has powerful psychological effects.
The same is true with churches. The numerical size of a church
is of more than statistical interest; it has some part in deter-
mining the status of a church in a country and therefore its
attitudes.

For example, where Christians are either a slight majority
or a very substantial minority of the total population, as in
Lebanon or Uganda, their position will always be rather
different from those countries where they are a very small
minority, as in most of Africa and Asia. In East Pakistan the
population is 55 million; of these 150,000 are Christians. In
Iran the population is 20 million; the total number of protestant
Christians is 3000. In Japan the population is more than 95
million; the total number of Christians is 700,000.

Similarly, a church will to some extent be influenced by
its numerical comparison with other churches in the same
country, even when all of them together form a minority of
the total population. Thus, the Anglican Church in Ceylon
and in Nigeria is the biggest of the non-Roman churches, and
therefore its condition and its outlook are different from

Anglican churches which are outnumbered by Presbyterians, as in Egypt and West Pakistan, or by Methodists, as in Ghana, or by Lutherans, as in Tanzania. Again, quite a lot will depend, even where the Church is a minority, on whether it is an educated minority, as in most African countries, with a considerable proportion of the leading men and women in all walks of life, or a largely uneducated minority, as in India and Pakistan, where most of the leaders are right outside the Christian community.

In trying to understand the Church across the world we should recognize that outside the West Christians are a minority everywhere except in the Philippines, Lebanon (?), and Uganda; and the vitality of a church is not related either to its size, its influence or its wealth.

This last point needs some consideration. The Church by its very nature is meant to expand.

> The universality of the Spiritual Community demands the function of expansion of churches. Since the universality of the Spiritual Community is implied in the confession of Jesus as the Christ, every church must participate in functions of expansion.[1]

It is alarming, then, to have to admit that some younger churches, like some older churches, have ceased to grow. The reasons for this are not discernible along sociological or economic lines. Thus, it appears to have nothing to do with the extent of religious liberty. In the Middle East, which is solidly Muslim, for example, there is a remarkable vitality in the two small churches in Iran (Presbyterian and Anglican) which have a constant trickle of Muslim converts annually. With other churches in the Middle East this is not so, though the difficulties in becoming a Christian in Iran are no less than in other Muslim countries of that area. In the Sudan there has been very strong pressure against missionary activity and in February 1964 some three hundred missionaries, Roman Catholic, Anglican and Presbyterian, were expelled from the three southern provinces. Nevertheless, in the face of every obstacle

[1] Paul Tillich, *Systematic Theology*, vol. III, Nisbet 1964, 205f.

to becoming a Christian and every inducement to becoming a Muslim, the Church in the Southern Sudan is growing fast. Anglicans number more than 100,000 and the rate of expansion is probably 10,000 a year. On the other hand in Sierra Leone there is complete religious liberty and the Anglican Church is not growing at all; if anything it is on the decline. We may take one further group of examples. There is no necessary relation between the size of financial grants and the growth of younger churches. In South America most of the Protestant churches have large grants from their sister churches in the United States, and they are all growing quite noticeably. But the Pentecostal churches, most of which are entirely in-digenous and have no help whatsoever from the United States either in money or missionaries, are growing at an astonish-ing rate, certainly faster than any other church in the world and probably faster than any other church in history. It is therefore a fallacy, and a very grave one, to assert that if only a church had more money or more missionaries or both, it would automatically grow. The examples above prove that this is manifestly not so.

How then do churches grow? This is a subject which has received a good deal of attention from Roland Allen and, more recently, from Donald McGavran.[1] In the past churches have grown faster in Africa and the Pacific islands than in Asia, and faster in tribal parts of Asia, for example among the Nagas, Karens, Bhils, than non-tribal. Conversions from animism have been easier, on the whole, than conversions from other religions.

Three factors seem to influence church growth in varying degrees. First, there is the primacy of evangelism. Where this ranks high in a church's programme expansion is more likely. We do not mean by this incessant evangelistic preaching with appeals for decision. We do mean a clear statement of the Gospel so that Christians know what they believe and why, and are thus better able to bear witness to Jesus Christ in their

[1] See R. Allen, *Missionary Methods: St Paul's or Ours?*, 1912, and *The Spontaneous Expansion of the Church*, 1927, and D. McGavran, *The Bridges of God*, 1955, and *How Churches Grow*, 1959—all published by World Dominion Press.

daily life. If churches are to grow significantly this depends almost entirely on the strength of lay witness. Where this happens there follows what Roland Allen calls 'spontaneous expansion' and what Donald McGavran calls 'a people's movement'. There have been notable examples of this in Uganda, South India and parts of Indonesia, as well as among the Maoris of New Zealand in the early days of mission to them. But the outstanding contemporary examples of this are to be seen in the Pentecostal churches of Brazil and Chile and the Plymouth Brethren in Argentina. In October 1963 on a visit to Brazil I met the leaders of some of these Pentecostal churches. At that date one had brought into being 227 congregations after nine years' work, another 480 congregations after seven years' work. Both churches, in addition to being wholly indigenous, lay tremendous emphasis on the power of each believer's personal testimony to Christ. In Chile this has resulted in Pentecostal groups numbering one million, more than 15 per cent of the population.

A second factor in church growth is an indigenous form of worship. This has played a strong part in the success of the Pentecostal churches in South America and also of the 'spiritual' or sect churches of West Africa, where there is a vigorous reaction in some circles against an imposed form of western worship. In Nigeria, Ghana and Sierra Leone English is the *lingua franca* and some of the sect churches actually worship in English. The reaction is not against the English language but against western forms and especially western restraint. If Christianity is to meet the needs of many people today a place will have to be found in its corporate worship for expressions of ecstasy once more.

A third necessary factor is a sense of welcoming fellowship. Christian *koinonia* can be either of the inclusive or exclusive type. In the East African revival it is largely exclusive, though strong and intense for those within. It is specifically a *revival* fellowship for those ready to undergo renewal on strict terms.[1]

[1] For fuller description see M. A. C. Warren, *Revival—an Enquiry*, SCM Press 1954, and Roy Hession, *The Calvary Road*, Christian Literature Crusade 1950.

The Pentecostal churches, however, are much more open and inclusive. They bestow on the outsider a sense of significance and of being wanted, and in South America, where Pentecostalism is at its purest and best, this provides immense potential for church growth. Unfortunately this is not the impression given by most other Christian congregations to outsiders.

McGavran believes that the Gospel should follow the line of response. He makes an important point which deserves much more attention by church leaders than it has received. Nevertheless, there must be exceptions to this theory. If the Church remained only where growth was visible and measurable it would contract out of most of the Muslim world and other areas such as rural Japan. Around the Arabian-Persian Gulf there are missionaries from the Reformed Church of the USA. Almost alone they have borne witness to Jesus Christ, but in eighty years of splendid work they have not seen eighty converts. Should the Church leave because as yet it has produced no people's movement or spontaneous expansion? Surely not. Irrespective of growth it is of enormous importance that there should be a Christian presence even in the most unresponsive places. What matters most in the fulfilment of mission is neither the size of a church nor its influence but the fact that there is some Christian presence, praying, loving, serving, and witnessing among non-Christan people, themselves at least the latent Church. One day the latent Church in every place will become manifest. Its true size will then be known—but it will then be irrelevant.

ENVIRONMENT

In the West there are at least the remains of Christendom; the influence of Christian civilization is still to be found in many commonly accepted standards of behaviour, even where we fall short of them. No historian or sociologist could deny that the Christian Gospel has left profound marks on the culture of Europe and North America. One has only to be in countries where there has been no such influence to notice the difference. If, for example, a driver is a Muslim of limited education, believing in *kismet* (fate), he will suppose that whether he has an accident or not will have been pre-ordained and therefore nothing he can do by way of care or responsibility will avert it. Take a taxi in Teheran and see! Similarly, in much of West Africa the only thing that you must in no circumstances kill on the roads is a duck. This is cold comfort for passengers and pedestrians alike.

However de-christianized the West has become the persistent influence of Jesus Christ, directly and indirectly, is still something to be reckoned with. Life in the West can never again be the same as it was, or as it still is in countries where he is barely known. It is easier to reject Christ than to forget him. It is interesting to see how many modern novelists, who make no Christian profession, not only write within a Christian mythological framework but somehow cannot leave Christ, the Church, and Christianity alone. The atmosphere of the West is different because of Jesus Christ, notwithstanding all the anti-Christian forces at work among us. He has affected our laws, our literature, our values, our systems of government, and prepared the way for the revolution of modern science and technology. It is Jesus Christ who has broken life open in such a way as to make it possible for men to be atheists and to allow them such freedom. He always insisted that men should be free to disbelieve. But no one's life in the West, believer or unbeliever, can escape the effects of Jesus Christ on his environment.

In Africa and Asia everything is different. The Church lives in a culture that has never been christianized from its centre outward, though in places it has to some extent been influenced and modified by the impact of Christianity as an external force. The difference between the cultural situations of East and West is much greater than those who have not experienced both can usually imagine. One consequence of this for the Church is that so much of what it tends to assume and take for granted and regard as its right in the West does not obtain outside the West.

Religion and culture, although distinct as concepts, are not easily separable, especially in the East. They tend to come in the same package. You cannot think of India without Hinduism or of the Arab world without Islam. Similarly, the early Christian missionaries, coming from the West, could not easily think of implanting Christianity without also implanting civilization as they understood it. Being men of their age they are not to be blamed for this. What they did was done with the highest motives. If David Livingstone in Central Africa and Alexander Mackay in Uganda and others like them had not been concerned with commerce and agriculture as well as with evangelization, they would have been denying the African the wholeness of the Gospel. The only commerce the chiefs knew was the slave trade conducted by the Arabs. If poverty was to be relieved and progress made, there had to be alternatives— and they introduced them by means of the only civilization and culture which they knew.[1] All this has inevitably led to a culture clash which has partly queered the pitch for the religious encounter. The Gospel has hardly been seen except in its western cultural dress, and it was probably impossible that it should have been otherwise. There were some notable exceptions such as Robert de Nobili (1577-1656), the great Jesuit missionary in India, and Adam Schall (1592-1666) and Matteo Ricci (1552-1610), Jesuit missionaries in China, and later James Hudson Taylor (1832-1905), founder of the China Inland Mission, and C. F. Andrews (1871-1940) of India, all of whom did their utmost to adapt themselves wholly to the customs and culture of the land and people they made their own. But these were exceptions. For the most part Christianity looked as western as commerce, industry and science, and its eastern origins were forgotten. One of the great problems of today for the churches in Africa and Asia is therefore to dewesternize their understanding of the Christian faith without at the same time diluting it. Only when there are enough in-

[1] For a fuller discussion of all this see Norman Goodall, *Christian Missions and Social Ferment*, Epworth Press 1964, chapters 1 and 2, and Roland Oliver, *The Missionary Factor in East Africa*, Longmans 1952, pp. 9ff.

digenous theologians in these churches will this task be properly and safely accomplished.

Nevertheless, the link between Christianity and western culture need not necessarily prove so disastrous as it has sometimes been held to be. Sooner or later in the expansive era of the nineteenth century all these lands would have been—as indeed they were—confronted with the trade and imperialist ambitions of the West. Is it not part of the pattern of Providence that they met the Gospel as well, and sometimes first of all? Today there is emerging a common culture, embracing all nations and stretching round the world. It is to be seen in the vast uniformity of airports, hotels, embassies, business houses, transport, newspapers, telecommunications, and the increasing use of the English language. This culture was nurtured in the West and drew on Christian sources, but it is now a purely secular culture largely devoid of religious foundation or attachment. The problem of the younger churches has therefore shifted. Their need is less to explain the past than to meet the present and to discover for themselves those forms of Christian life and witness which are called for in the remarkably mixed cultures in which they are now set. For something of the old will certainly be retained and mingled with the new. The most striking example of this is Japan, perhaps the most progressive of all non-western countries, highly westernized in so many respects and yet retaining a devoted hold on its own past, as in some of the ceremonies and in dress. In West Africa also there is a good deal of westernization, but at the same time reaction from this, and it is witnessed in the recent delight and pride in African dress, in the unearthing of their own history and the large numbers of secret societies.

Cultures as well as individuals have to be baptized into Christ. It is at this point that the Gospel often seems unrelated and irrelevant to the young intellectuals and the more sophisticated classes of African and Asian countries. It is a matter of great urgency for the churches to work out their relation both to the traditional and the changing cultures and to show that it is no more necessary for a Christian to become westernized—unless he has to be for vocational or professional reasons—than it was for a Christian to be circumcised and so made a Jew, as St Paul saw so clearly. But this is something that indigenous churches must eventually do for themselves; it cannot be done for them by their western friends.

Except in India most educated Christians are extremely westernized. In some countries, such as Japan, their own theologians show far more interest in western theology than in relating the faith to their own traditions. In Bangalore and Ibadan there are Christian Institutes for the Study of Religion and Society, and similar study centres are growing up elsewhere. Their importance is beyond exaggeration if the Church is to adapt in the right way to its environment. There can be no evangelism without understanding, and this means the finding of talking points and areas of common concern, the creating of neutral ground where Christians and men of other faiths can meet and talk openly and freely in a situation of mutual respect. The Church in every place *has to* come to terms with its cultural environment. In much of Africa and Asia this has hardly been begun as yet. The issue is enormous, for 'not only Jews but also Greeks and Romans, medievalists and moderns, Westerners and Orientals, have rejected Christ because they saw in him a threat to their culture'.[1] It is important today that he should be seen not only as the one who more than all others influenced western culture at its best, but also as the one who is its sternest judge and critic. For he is less within culture than above it, and it is high time that the eternal Christ, who has been encountered mostly as the western Christ, shall be seen and known without his western clothes.

Arnold Toynbee urges a reconsideration of the Jesuits' approach, because they tried

> to disengage Christianity from the non-Christian ingredients in the Western civilization and to present Christianity to the Hindus and to the Chinese, not as the local religion of the West, but as a universal religion with a message for all mankind. The Jesuits stripped Christianity of its accidental and irrelevant

[1] Richard Niebuhr, *Christ and Culture*, Faber 1952, 20.

Western accessories, and offered the essence of it to China in a Chinese, and to India in a Hindu, intellectual and literary dress in which there was no incongruous Western embroidery to jar on Asian sensibilities.[1]

The Jesuits' lack of success was not due to a wrong policy but to internal divisions in the Roman Catholic Church. This was 350 years ago. It is too late in most places for western churches to initiate or imitate this policy because they are no longer in a position to call the tune. The younger churches of Africa and Asia will themselves have to decide what to take and what to leave and how to relate the changeless Gospel of Jesus Christ to their own rapidly changing countries and cultures.

SECURITY

In the West the Church still has great social, economic and cultural security. This may be a good deal less than fifty years ago, but in comparison with Africa and the East it is still considerable. The Church in the West has wealth and property in varying degrees. It has prestige and, in some countries, privilege. No one is disqualified from a high position because of his church affiliation, and in the United States he can be helped to high office by belonging to a church, especially the 'right' church.[2] A Christian is not all that different from his neighbours. He will not normally be persecuted or disregarded because of his beliefs and practices. But in Asia it can be a great disadvantage to personal promotion in the secular world to be a Christian; and in Africa, where Christianity is not merely tolerated but often warmly welcomed and highly respected, to live by Christian standards in the sphere of politics and administration of the law can lead to grave difficulties and possible privation. This has already happened both in South Africa and in Ghana.

It is true, of course, that in these less happy situations the Church is much closer to the early Church than it can ever be

---

[1] Arnold Toynbee, *The World and the West*, OUP 1953, 64.
[2] See Vance Packard, *The Status Seekers*, Pelican 1961, 173-183.

in the contemporary West. And it is easier to learn what it means to be the Church in contexts where it is more sharply differentiated from the secular world. In the West our security too often lies in the wrong place—in Parliament, democracy, public opinion, endowments. One of the things that the Church is learning in some communist countries, particularly East Germany, is that the only real security is in God, the Lord of history and of history's lords, and not in state protection or in any form of privilege.

In a recent book we have been able to hear Christian voices out of East Germany. Here is one of them:

> We have learnt that there is no need to be afraid of the Communist. He may treat us like second-class citizens and restrict us in many of our plans and activities, but we have something he has not—freedom of belief. What we do have to be afraid of is sterility within the church, and of the possibility that the church might die of causes within itself! So it is not the church we try to preserve now, but the Gospel. Preserving the Gospel means living the Gospel, and living the Gospel means pro-existence—being there for the world, just as Christ was there for the world.

Here is a quite new perspective to thinking about the Church, and it comes out of a Marxist country. They are not worried about what the state may do to them or take from them; they have seen what the apostles also saw so clearly, that the Church's chief dangers are from inside and not from outside. Perhaps it is only when all other freedoms which we take for granted are removed that we discover fully the meaning of true Christian freedom. Here is another voice:

> A church which complains about the present and agonizes about the future is failing to sing the praises of its Lord to the world.[1]

These are brave words coming out of a church which has forfeited most of its former securities. Stripped of these it is

[1] *Pro-Existence: Christian Voices in East Germany*, edited by Elisabeth Adler, SCM Press 1964, pp. 13, 114.

learning what Bonhoeffer meant in his phrase 'Christ existing as his church'.

This is the kind of situation in which some of the younger churches may soon find themselves. China is not likely to be the only one for long. As a preparation for such a time some understanding of the theology of opposition is an imperative.

In the New Testament, and in almost every book, it is made clear that the Church is to expect a hard time with antagonism continuing to the end. 'In the world you have tribulation; but be of good cheer, I have overcome the world' (John 16.33 RSV). Most of the many references to suffering do not refer to sickness but to persecution. Sometimes this would be brought about by local officials or the mob; sometimes, especially later, it would be state policy ruthlessly carried out. The early Church took this for granted as its lot. But we should notice certain things about their attitude.

First, Christians were taught by the apostles to respect the government and obey its laws (Rom. 13.1; Tit. 3.1; I Pet. 2.13-14). This is obviously an important principle for every Christian community to accept. The East German Christians quoted above write about their political leaders with restraint and charity, realizing that they must not be held in contempt, because they are instruments in the hand of God. Second, all rulers and governments are to be prayed for, irrespective of their religious or political affiliations (I Tim. 2.1, 2). It is unbiblical and therefore regrettable that in the Prayer for the Church in the Anglican Holy Communion service, and in many of its revisions, we qualify this and pray only for 'all Christian Kings, Princes and Governors'. They need prayer not because they are Christians or non-Christians but because they are in positions of leadership and responsibility with the fortunes of many people in their power. Third, St Paul was prepared to appeal to the government against injustice (Acts 25.11)—it was not a Christian government; such considerations are irrelevant. Fourth, St Paul never courted persecution and he did not seek for martyrdom. He left a city when things became too hot for him and in Damascus he was let down from the wall in a basket to escape (II Cor. 11.32ff). Fifth, if

D

it came to the point of conflict and Christians had to make a
personal decision on some course of action, they had to obey
God rather than men (Acts 4.19), and these became the chief
occasions for suffering and arousing opposition. They were
under an obligation to preach the Gospel and give their witness whatever the consequences. There was something irre-
pressible about this apostolic Church which we lack today.
But this obligation to preach and witness, even at the risk of
incurring opposition, is one of the points where many contemporary churches are hardly in the apostolic succession
when things are hard.

Because we have been conditioned by 1600 years of post-
Constantinian Christendom, we are shocked that anyone
should oppose the Church and its claims and its servants. We
are shocked in the name of the very civilization which the
Gospel has created. But Islam of course is equally shocked and
affronted that any single man or woman of its close-knit house-
hold should ever defect into the Christian Church. In the
Muslim world the Church therefore has always had to face
opposition, at least since the disastrous Crusades, the effects
of which still live on. Elsewhere and until recently the Church
has had little tough opposition except in the very early years
of persecution which most newly-founded churches had for
a brief spell after the modern missionary movement began.
This means that from their parent churches in the West the
younger churches have subtly acquired the attitude that the
Christian life is a safe and not a dangerous thing, that the
Church should be left in peace by the State, and that in any
case the Church should not take risks which would make it
unpopular. There are notable exceptions, but as an attitude
it is reflected in one of the Anglican collects which prays 'that
the course of this world may be so peaceably ordered by thy
governance, that thy Church may joyfully serve thee in all
godly quietness' (Trinity V). We should ask whether this is a
right and a realistic prayer to use today, and whether the
early Church ever expected to be allowed to serve in godly
quietness. Such presuppositions of praying and thinking have
been imposed on the churches of Africa and Asia by the West,

presuppositions very far removed from those of the apostolic Church.

Dr Visser 't Hooft has given us a more sensible perspective on all this by reminding us that

> the normal situation is rather the situation of open conflict. Must we not look on the period from roughly the middle of the nineteenth to the middle of the twentieth century as a sort of armistice period in the relations between missions and the world? The contradiction of the world was more or less *sotto voce* and there was sufficient outside encouragement so as not to notice these negative voices. The encouragement which came from the world, and sometimes even from the Church, was often given for the wrong reasons. Somehow missions seemed to become an accepted part of modern civilization.[1]

We should remember too that in the field of politics today there are many prisoners who are prisoners of conscience. Nehru, Nkrumah, Nkomo, and others were all once in prison, and not for religious reasons. In a world where men will go to prison for their political activity and belief—as in the South African Treason Trial—ought there not to be some who are willing to go there because of their Christian witness and their refusal to conform to the state when it tries to suppress this? It is in the younger churches of Africa and Asia where this more costly form of witness will soon have to be borne, because it is there that the opposition is becoming fiercer than in the western democracies. One of the few remaining roles of the western missionary may be to prepare the churches in some of these countries to live under totalitarian rule of some kind and 'not to be surprised at the fiery ordeal which comes upon you to prove you, as though something strange were happening to you' (I Peter 4.12 RSV). For 'all who desire to live a godly life in Christ Jesus will be persecuted' (II Tim. 3.12 RSV).

In so brief a compass it is a risk to write about the exciting changes and the massive problems facing the younger churches. Much has to be omitted; understanding is always limited; im-

[1] *Witness in Six Continents*, ed. R. K. Orchard, Edinburgh House Press 1964, p. 24.

pressions given may be unintentionally wrong. But in a book
of this kind it is a risk that has to be taken. The reason we
take it is to attempt some kind of interpretation of their
situation and their needs. The way these needs are to be met
may be very different in the future, especially if churches are
cut off from free contact with their parent churches, as in
Cuba and the Sudan, and even their neighbouring churches, as
in China. When this happens the only help that is open to all
to give is that of intercession based on sympathetic love, and
a few laymen, not missionaries, serving in these countries in
secular vocations will be our sole personal links.

But those who believe firmly in Jesus Christ will not lose
heart about his Church, for it is he who builds it himself and
it is he who said that 'the forces of death shall never over-
power it' (Matt. 16.18).

4

THE MISSION AND THE PASSION
A Way of Living

MISSION sooner or later leads into passion. In biblical categories—and these remain contemporary—the servant must
suffer, the world being what it is. Three short preliminary
points will introduce this theme.

Isaiah wrote much about the servant of God and in four
famous poems he speaks of his mission and his suffering (Isa.
42.1-4; 49.1-6; 50.4-9; 52.13–53.12). The progression from the
one to the other is illuminating. In the first song the servant's
character and mission are described. He is God's chosen and
has his Spirit; he is gentle and patient. His mission is to bring
forth justice to the nations. In the second song the servant's
calling is said to be from the womb, his mouth is like a sharp
sword, and in him God is to be glorified. His mission is 'to
bring Jacob back to God', but this is extended, for 'it is too
light a thing that you should be my servant to raise up the
tribes of Jacob and to restore the preserved of Israel; I will give
you as a light to the nations, that my salvation may reach to
the end of the earth'. In the third song the theme changes from
the servant's mission to his passion. 'I gave my back to the
smiters, and my cheeks to those who pulled out the beard;
I hid not my face from shame and spitting.' And in the fourth
song the passion theme is developed in some of the best known
and most moving descriptions of suffering in all literature. He
is despised, rejected, acquainted with sorrow and grief, stricken,
afflicted, wounded, bruised, oppressed, silent, pouring out his
soul to death, numbered with sinners, bearing sin, making
intercession. Mission leads into passion. Passion is not only the
result but in some respects the climax of mission; it is that

which makes mission effective. This at least is the message of
Isaiah 53.

When Jesus sent the Twelve out on their mission he warned
them of the possibility that instead of being welcomed and
received they might be rejected. 'If any place will not receive
you and they refuse to hear you . . .' (Mark 6.11 RSV). He
said: 'Remember the word that I said to you, "A servant is not
greater than his master." If they persecuted me, they will persecute you' (John 15.20 RSV). There is a congruity of pattern
right through. The prophets were rejected; the Messiah was
rejected; his apostles would be rejected. And the irony is that
it is the people of God who join in the rejecting. They are
rejected by Jews as much as by Gentiles, by the Church as
much as by the world. At the heart of mission there is always
a cross.

Both these themes, mission and passion, are brought together in one of our Lord's great sayings. 'The Son of man
came not to be ministered unto, but to minister'—there is the
mission—'and to give his life as a ransom for many'—there is
the passion (Mark 10.45). Mission always involves the giving of
life, though not necessarily in death, but invariably in some
form of sacrifice. The servant 'poured out his soul unto death'
(Isa. 53.12). The good shepherd 'lays down his life for the
sheep' (John 10.11, 15). Paul writes: 'Even if I am to be poured
as a libation upon the sacrificial offering of your faith, I am
glad and rejoice with you all' (Phil. 2.17 RSV).

Sooner or later, then, every form of mission leads to some
form of cross. The very shape of mission is cruciform. We can
understand mission only in terms of the Cross. One of the
factors about being a missionary today in any country, including the West, is the new forms of suffering to which he is
exposed. Formerly, in the case of overseas missionaries, the
sufferings and the danger were largely physical, especially
arising from tropical diseases. Today there is much less physical
risk, but there is great psychological and spiritual strain which
makes up the cross for the missionary, especially the foreign
missionary, whose foreignness adds to the weight of his cross.
We shall be examining this, but before doing so it is important

first to look at certain aspects of the passion theme in the New Testament.

ABOUT BEARING

The Bible has a lot to say about this, and the New Testament uses a variety of Greek verbs which are translated as 'bear' or 'carry' or 'take away'. Consider, simply as a group of verses, the following:

Behold, the Lamb of God, who takes away the sin of the world (John 1.29).

He himself bore our sins in his body on the tree (I Peter 2.24).

Whoever does not bear his own cross and come after me, cannot be my disciple (Luke 12.27).

I bear on my body the marks of Jesus (Gal. 6.17).

We who are strong ought to bear with the failings of the weak (Rom. 15.1).

He took our infirmities and bore our diseases (Matt. 8.17; cf. Isa. 53.4).

Bear one another's burdens (Gal. 6.2). [RSV]

From this little cluster of texts two closely linked ideas would seem to emerge. First, the cross is something which has to be borne, whether it be Christ's or the Christian's. Second, there is a relation between the Cross and everything that we have to bear. If we pursue the study of what has to be borne by those who engage in mission today, and if we can trace the resemblances between what makes up the cross for us and what made up the cross for Jesus, we shall have gone some way into our subject.

The Cross is both an event and a principle. As an event it is unique and once for all, lying at the heart of the Christian Gospel. But it is more than an event, as Jesus made clear when he told his disciples that they too would have to bear a cross —and most of them were not crucified. In this context he is using the expression metaphorically. The cross belongs to the whole structure of the Christian faith, life, and mission. Discipleship means cross-bearing. The cross is a basic principle in Christianity: it is the way it works and the way it works itself out. The world which crucified Jesus could be expected to deal roughly with his friends. There was to be a resemblance of pattern, if in a variety of keys, all the way through. 'If the world hates you, know that it has hated me before it hated you' (John 15.18). 'If they persecuted me, they will persecute you' (John 15.20 RSV). The more the Christian plunges into mission, so much the more he plunges into passion. 'As the Father has sent me, even so I send you' (John 20.21 RSV)—and this is what it may mean. It was not accidental that the early Christian word for a witness (Greek *martus*) was soon to acquire a new sense and to be transliterated as martyr, so combining the ideas of mission and suffering. To witness in this kind of world will issue in suffering.

Clearly then the Cross itself is not unique. The uniqueness of Calvary does not consist in the Cross but in the Crucified and what he achieved on the cross. Two thieves were crucified on identical crosses, as thousands have been before and since. The same sort of thing happens endlessly and the pattern is repeated again and again. Variations on the passion theme are constantly being worked out. In a remarkable and evocative book F. W. Dillistone takes four celebrated novels whose central concern is redemptive suffering: Mauriac's *The Lamb*, Melville's *Billy Bud*, Nikos Kazantzakis's *Christ Recrucified*, and Faulkner's *A Fable*.[1] Dillistone's interpretation of the first of these is specially helpful for our purpose. The story is about a sacrifice, a death, which brought about reconciliation and peace. At the end one of the characters says: 'Yes, I know that love does exist in the world. But it is crucified in the world and we with it.' On this Dillistone comments:

So we are brought back to Mauriac's central message—that whensoever and wheresoever the sufferings of Christ are reproduced in one of his servants, there salvation is being worked out; the salvation both of the sufferer and those for whom he is

[1] F. W. Dillistone, *The Novelist and the Passion Story*, Collins 1960.

suffering. Christ's act is supreme, definitive, unapproachable. Yet it cannot be effective in the world today unless it is brought near through its re-enactment in the lives of saintly figures such as Xavier.[1]

Liturgically this re-enactment of the passion in dramatic form takes place in the Eucharist. It is also meant to take place in the life and witness of the Church and of individual Christians in the secular world. Life's real altars are *outside* church buildings. They are the places in the world where Christians get maltreated and misunderstood and sometimes mocked because they are Christians. When this happens to men and women anywhere, they are having a tiny glimpse and share of the passion of the Lord. Mission leads into passion. The cross is all about bearing. It is a principle as well as an event. It has to be re-enacted time and again in some form or other as Christians give their witness, for this can be more articulate than words. In this world the cross is an inevitable consequence of effective mission, for it is the world protesting against the love and truth of God; it is the world preferring darkness to light because its deeds are evil. 'The Cross as an event is no artificial scheme. It is what happens when a love like Christ's encounters a world like Jerusalem.'[2]

THE COMPOSITION OF THE CROSS

If we can grasp that the Cross is not merely an event, even for Jesus, but a whole pattern of experiences, of humility and patience, of obedience and disappointment, of suffering and sacrifice, we shall see that it is operative right through his ministry. The actual cross on which he died is the great climax to a whole series of circumstances which, taken together, came to compose that cross. Jesus accepted the cross as a principle long before he accepted it as a deed at Calvary. It was laid upon him from the beginning. From his birth onwards the cross in all its cruelty and injustice was straining to grasp and encircle

[1] Op. cit., 44.
[2] K. Cragg, *The Call of the Minaret*, OUP 1956, 298.

and destroy him through the tentacles of history. It started with Herod and the massacre of the baby boys. It happened again at Nazareth after his first sermon when he announced the manifesto of his ministry, and 'the whole congregation were infuriated. They leapt up, threw him out of the town, and took him to the brow of the hill on which it was built, meaning to hurl him over the edge' (Luke 4.28f). It continued even in the gay weeks of the early Galilean ministry, where Mark groups together five conflict stories which culminate in the Pharisees and Herodians consulting together about how they could destroy him (Mark 3.6). Gradually the shadow of the cross falls more darkly over his path and he alludes to it specifically in private conversation with the disciples in the well-known passion sayings (Mark 8.31; 9.31; 10.33, 45, etc.). He knows it is inevitable. The cross is being composed and constructed by the various cross-currents that run up against him. For the cross is more than two pieces of wood nailed together cross-wise. That is merely the material symbol of the moral and spiritual cross that Jesus bore and that we have to bear after him.

What are the basic things, the ingredients, which actually made up our Lord's cross and led him to it? We may discern four, all of which play a decisive part in the passion narrative: the government, the ecclesiastical hierarchy, the mob, and Judas Iscariot. The government gave its permission and endorsed a miscarriage of justice; the chief priests and Jewish leaders had plotted against Jesus all along and finally they got their way; the multitude, whipped up by professional agitators, shouted 'Crucify him'; and Judas was responsible for the act which delivered Jesus into the hands of his enemies. So the cross of Jesus was made for him by the state, the church, the people, and a friend. These are still the powers which create innumerable crosses today for those engaged on mission. We will consider them at work in their modern setting. Over the years by visits to churches in different lands and conversation with many missionaries and observation of others, I have collected a great deal of material on this subject. It would obviously be improper and unwise in presenting the illustrations that follow to do so in such a way that they would be too easily recognizable. But all of them are true and within my personal knowledge. These four factors can be found in every part of the world today, creating resistance to those involved in the Christian mission, leading them into some sort of passion.

Government Injustice. The Roman government, represented in the Province of Judaea by Pontius Pilate, the Procurator, had no official interest in a Jewish religious teacher. Judaism was one of the permitted religions of the Empire, even if held in contempt. In government eyes Jesus was small fry, hardly significant. Provided people did not take too much notice of him and provided he did not stir up any kind of trouble or disturb the peace, he could be safely ignored. There had been others. But if he became the centre of a popular movement in any way critical of the government, if he spoke of any other king, any other authority than Caesar's, he might prove a dangerous threat and would need to be suppressed or got rid of. And it was a foreign government.

The Roman Empire, under whose rule Jesus lived, had a deserved reputation for justice. Its concern was to maintain law and order and to preserve peace. On the whole it did this successfully. But in a distant province a long way from Rome expediency could sometimes override justice, as in the trial of Jesus. Pilate, having declared him innocent, delivers him to be crucified so that the Jews may have their own way and the people do what they like with him.

In the eyes of African or Asian governments missionaries today are small fry—and they are usually foreigners. In newly independent countries, where the careers of politicians are often precarious, where bribery and corruption are often rampant, and where inefficiency can sometimes be intolerable and beyond belief, the presence of foreigners, though a necessity, is often an embarrassment. And the presence of foreign missionaries, unless they are economically productive, can be highly resented. One of the ironies of our time is that just when world travel is easier than ever before from the point of

view of transport, many countries, which need both tourists
and technical help of all kinds from overseas, are making it
more and more difficult for visitors to get in. Visas, photos,
customs declarations, exchange regulations, letters of entry,
often in triplicate or worse, are required in many places, and
it can take up to an hour or even more to get past the various
officials in ports and airports. But this is by the way and a
relatively minor, if irritating, matter. At least it can represent
the first experience of a cross and some of its splinters to a
visitor or missionary on his arrival.

Many new countries still have a reputation for justice,
especially in their high courts, though judges can sometimes be
harried by governments, as we have seen under the white
nationalism of South Africa and the black nationalism of
Ghana. But at the lower levels justice cannot always be
secured. Often witnesses refuse to give evidence and run away;
others accept payment to give false evidence. When a foreigner, whether he is a missionary or not, becomes unpopular
for some reason, he can be accused on some trumped-up
charge and either imprisoned or deported. There have been a
number of such cases in Africa. In one African country a
missionary was falsely accused of certain acts; he was held in
custody and questioned but not allowed to contact his solicitor.
Discredit was brought upon him by false accusations and he
had to leave. A probable reason for this particular injustice
was that a certain African official, now in a position of authority, had several years ago been dismissed from a job by this
missionary for a serious misdemeanour and was now getting
his own back. It is not of course only foreigners who suffer in
this way; many Africans also suffer. I have personally known
some who have spent their life-savings in court cases attempt-
ing to secure justice for themselves or their relatives or their
property, but they have lost because their opponent was a
richer man and could bribe the magistrates or the counsel.

Today in certain African countries a casual criticism of the
head of state or some powerful politician can be taken as an
insult. A missionary—and indeed any foreigner—can be expelled for nothing more than this, possibly on the evidence of

someone with a personal grudge against him. Jesus respected
the government; he did not criticize it. On the only occasion
when he was invited to do so he gave an answer which was
not merely a superlative piece of diplomacy but also a classic
statement of a great principle about the respective claims of
God and the state upon man. Nevertheless, he was still used
as a pawn in the power game and as a scapegoat for the Jewish
nationalism which he himself had condemned. He died at the
hands of the Romans because to them he was a nationalist. He
died at the hands of the Jews because to them he had refused
to be a nationalist. 'It is expedient that one man should die
for the people' had been the advice of Caiaphas (John 11.50).
Missionaries in some places have likewise provided governments with scapegoats, just as Nero accused the Christians of
starting the great fire of Rome. Being a missionary is a dangerous occupation. Few others are so vulnerable, however
neutral they remain, and there are some situations where
neutrality is sin, as Trevor Huddleston and others found in
Johannesburg. Similarly, Africans can be in even worse trouble
if they do not identify themselves wholly with what in some
places is a fanatical and an idolatrous nationalism. Their
loyalty to the mission of Christ and to a Church, which because
it is catholic can never be nationalist, can create for them a
cross and a passion. Christians, national or foreign, missionary
or non-missionary, can be blamed and dealt with, if they are
popular and acceptable in any group of people for whom the
government is unpopular. This has been the case with the
Nagas of India, the Karens of Burma, and among the Bantu
tribes of the Southern Sudan.

But there are many other ways in which governments can
create crosses. Most missionaries have only a small salary,
usually but not always sufficient for them to live on but with
little left over. They are missionaries because they want to
serve the country and the people to whom they go. But this is
no longer regarded as heroic by some types of official and
even missionaries can be asked for bribes by customs officials
in some countries. In one West African country a certain
missionary had to do a difficult journey of 600 miles three

times because the customs officials would not clear his luggage at the port. The only reason for this was that he was unwilling to bribe them. The missionary had come to serve their people and given up much in order to do so, but this made no difference. Drugs, medicines, surgical appliances are constantly needed by mission hospitals throughout the world. They are expensive and supplies of these are often bought through generous voluntary gifts of missionary supporters in the West. In Africa or Asia they are being used solely for the benefit and health of millions of people and they save countless lives. Nevertheless, although given and sent with no other purpose, such is the stupidity of officialdom and government regulations in some countries that not only can these goods be held up for weeks in customs but can even be heavily taxed.

It can be dangerous for missionaries to be too successful or popular. In one part of East Africa a young missionary agriculturist and his wife created a magnificent group farm. They worked extremely hard, using imagination and skill, clearing bush and growing food where nothing edible had ever grown before. They triumphed over every setback—and there were many. They had no personal ambition except to serve and they wanted nothing for themselves. After two years they had twenty-seven families farming on a communal basis; they had a fine herd of cattle; they grew all the food they needed and were entirely self-supporting. They had in fact produced a model communal farm and their one desire was to hand this over to the senior African and to repeat the same experiment elsewhere. But officials who had previously backed them became jealous of their success, for they had achieved something that none of the nationals could possibly have achieved at that stage of development, and permission for them to remain at work in that country was withdrawn.

At the time of writing this chapter another agricultural missionary in a West African country is having constant obstacles put in his way by government servants. For many years he has fought a lonely battle trying to help some of the thousands of unemployed ex-school-boys by teaching them to farm in their own villages instead of going to the towns and joining the queues of the jobless or the gangs of the delinquent. It took years of work and persuasion before the government would recognize the importance of agriculture and he had one difficulty and disappointment after another. At last the idea caught on; the value of his work was seen and help provided. Now relatively inexperienced government officials interfere with the missionary who started the scheme, and some have been doing their utmost to discredit him by trying to find false accusations against him. Why? This is part of the mystery of the Cross, the special cross that comes to some missionaries today. There are no easy answers to the Why of the Cross, except that it is made by man whose heart is perverse and desperately wicked.

In one of India's most famous colleges I once met a distinguished woman missionary who was head of the history department. With some thirty years of service and experience behind her and a mind still open to new ideas, she was doing a wonderful job. For most of that time she had been allowed considerable independence and freedom of initiative in the way she ran the department and taught her subject on which she was an expert. But shortly before my visit the education authorities of the state in which the college was functioning introduced a series of new regulations and a great deal of red tape. The regulations were to a great extent impractical, the work of doctrinaire theorists who had never had to teach, and the red tape was exasperating as it involved time and energy which could have been so much better spent. For an experienced and conscientious teacher, whether expatriate or a national, this is very frustrating and irritating. The missionary could of course have packed her bags and gone home; she had every right to, having borne the heat and burden of a long day. How easily she could have refused to put up with the nonsense of the newly created situation with which she profoundly disagreed. But the missionary also had to consider the young men who were depending on her for their teaching and whom she would fail if she went home because life had become more difficult. The missionary chose to stay, and in doing this chose also a cross—the cross of frustration. This is a choice, a cross, for many missionaries in most countries under present circumstances.

The principal of one of the best-known schools in a certain West African country left for another post. A succession of distinguished and dedicated men had given that school an international reputation; some had been missionaries, some Africans, all had been Christians. The normal procedure when a vacancy occurred was for the governing body of the school to meet and eventually to appoint a suitable successor. A few weeks before my last visit to that country its president had overruled the board of governors, deprived them of their rights, and appointed the new principal himself, choosing a man from his party machine, a politician with no experience of teaching or education whatever. The missionaries on the staff were naturally dismayed and indignant; so were many of the Africans. What is the missionary to do? If he stays he has to sacrifice some of his professional integrity; if he goes he lets down a whole generation of boys whom he loves and wants to help. The Africans, of course, have no such choice, unless they opt for unemployment. Is it in keeping with the missionary calling and character to clear off when things get hard? This is the kind of situation and choice which creates a cross for the missionary in one place after another.

There is the cross of infinite patience and drudgery which also has to be accepted by some. I once had to visit a country with an Arab government which had very strict entry regulations. My visa had been applied for more than four months ahead of my visit, but not until forty-eight hours before I was due to fly from London did a cable come to say that it had at last been obtained. Only after I arrived did I realize the cost and effort expended in procuring that visa. The missionary who was responsible for administrative matters had been to the foreign office daily for several weeks. Each time he had had a long wait, sometimes of two or three hours, before he could see an official qualified to deal with his business. When at last he succeeded in getting an interview he would be told to come the next day. This just went on and on; sometimes he would see a different official, sometimes the same. Finally, another foreigner, whose chief advantage was that he was not a European, spent two whole mornings in the passport office and at last got the necessary visa. This was not all. My assignment was to minister to the clergy in a distant part of the interior which was a closed district and for which a special entry permit was always required. The missionary responsible for administration in the provincial capital of that area had to do the same thing day after day in order to get this permission. Exactly two minutes before the dead-line, after which it would have been too late, permission was cabled through to the air-terminal where I was waiting. Three highly qualified and very busy men had between them spent hundreds of hours waiting and waiting in order that I might visit that church for a month and help its pastors. This was their cross. The two missionaries, both graduates, had originally gone out to teach. As the internal situation worsened they had to undertake the much more difficult work of administration. What they did for me was no isolated piece of work. This was their daily chore. They had to do this for every incoming missionary, for every outgoing missionary, for every visiting bishop. Notwithstanding their being gifted teachers, their part in the Christian mission was to do the work of office boys, to be kept waiting for hours, for days, for weeks, to keep on going back, always to be polite and patient. If either of them had once lost his temper or made a fuss he would have been sent out of the country, and that might have meant all the other missionaries following. This daily drudgery was their part of the Cross, their entry into our Lord's passion. 'Yet he opened not his mouth.'

A married couple went as missionaries to this same country. The man was a literature worker, his wife a hospital sister-tutor. They had a house in the hospital compound. The time came when hospitals were nationalized and missionaries forbidden to work in them. In this particular hospital there was a serious shortage of trained staff, no full-time doctor on the premises and no sufficiently qualified sister. On some occasions there were patients critically ill and in extreme pain but no one available to treat them. The missionary sister, unemployed, had to live with this situation, powerless to intervene, not even allowed to lend a hand or soothe a sufferer, and yet to be in the same compound. If she had entered the hospital where she once had charge, she and her husband would have committed a grave offence and would probably have been expelled. Others elsewhere have had similar experiences. It is the kind of cross that Mary had to bear, standing by all the suffering and pain and being unable to do anything but watch helplessly. This is the passion some missionaries have had to enter.

In South Africa all who accept the New Testament doctrine that in Christ all men are one, whatever their colour or race, have to carry a perpetually heavy cross laid on them by the government policy of apartheid. For the Africans and the Coloureds this means a constant sense of degradation and inferiority. For the Whites with a conscience it means the agony of relationships in which an element of strain can seldom be absent. There is naught for their comfort whichever race they happen to be. It is a crime for white people to have an African sleeping under the same roof and vice versa.

These are a few examples of the various kinds of cross those engaged on mission in some parts of the world have laid upon them by government. And every day there is the cross of being misunderstood.

An Unwelcoming Church. Just as Jesus was crucified by order of a governor in an empire most famed for justice, so he was rejected by the people most noted for religious purity and zeal—the Jews. The Cross for Jesus was composed by the sheer unfaithfulness of his own Church; it was a cross of the bitterest disappointment. Jesus stands for a disappointed God, for God rejected by his people.

What more was there to do for my vineyard
   that I have not done in it?
When I looked for it to yield grapes,
   why did it yield wild grapes? (Isa 5.4).

O my people, what have I done to you?
   In what have I wearied you? (Mic. 6.3).

He came to his own home, and his own people received
him not (John 1.11 RSV).

He himself re-tells Isaiah's parable of the vineyard, extend-
ing the story and giving it a new point. The owner, who has
a beloved son, expects that the tenants will reverence his son
even though they ill-treated his servants. But when he sends
him, they say 'This is the heir; come, let us kill him'—and
they did so (Mark 12.6-8). This parable describes something of
the Lord's feelings about Israel. The people on whom God had
lavished so much love, to whom he had sent kings and judges,
prophets and wise men, were about to reject him, God's Son.
They were going to refuse his mission. The supreme pain of
the crucifixion was surely this moral anguish of being rejected.
Is anything in the world more hurtful than rejection by those
one loves? Christ's cross and passion stand for this rejection.
He died because the Jewish church could not take his message
or accept his standards. It was the church that took the
initiative in deciding that Jesus must die.

We must be careful here, for no parallel can be exact. Jesus
came as the Lord and Saviour of the Church and for him the
contrast between holiness and sin was a far more terrible
reality than it is for us. We, who take some part in his continuing mission, are sinful products of a sinful church, and
we go from one sinful church to another. It is not for us to give
the churches marks in grading their faithfulness and their
merits. But most missionaries are in for a shock and a
traumatic experience when they discover certain things in
the younger churches. And the shock is mutual. For Africans
and Asians are equally shocked when they discover certain
things about missionaries and about the churches in the West
from which they come. None must allow himself to think that
the church he is sent to is worse than the church he comes
from. This kind of judgment belongs to God alone. Rather
must we recognize that the churches from which we come
suffer from different kinds of weakness and fall into different
kinds of sin from the churches to which we may have to
go.

Thus, money played its part in putting Jesus on the cross. The church bribed Judas to betray him. It also bribed the guards and soldiers to tell a lie after his resurrection (Matt. 28.11-14). The wrong use of money and an overwhelming desire for it by whatever means can create a painful cross for some who serve in the younger churches. Bribery has not yet been stamped out. Quarrels between Christians and a certain incapacity to believe and to see spiritual truths are part of the scene. Litigation in the courts between Christians is one of the major problems and blemishes of the Church in India. In some parts of Africa an inordinate amount of the pastors' time is spent in settling quarrels when they visit their village congregations. On occasions when new appointments have to be made, particularly of bishops and others in positions of power, very often the decisive factor will not be a man's ability for the job but his tribe or his caste or his race. This is how the people of God still behave. But this is how they behaved when Jesus lived among men. His chosen disciples quarrelled about status and position, and to Nicodemus, a teacher in Israel, our Lord expressed surprise at his inability to understand a spiritual principle. But these are small crosses which the people of God make for one another.

The much harder cross is that of being rejected. Israel had longed for Jesus, praying for their Messiah through the centuries. When he came he was too much for them and they refused him. Most churches, at least through the mouths of their leaders, long for missionaries, praying for them and asking for them. But when the missionaries arrive they often find that they are not really welcome or wanted. They have to accept this curious contradiction at the heart of a church's life: they have to be in the position of being needed but not wanted. In 1963 the first All Africa Church Conference was held in Kampala, Uganda. A missionary in Uganda, who attended it, wrote later:

'It meant a certain amount of speaking against missionaries as "foreigners" and "agents of the colonialists". But on balance they came down on the side of still wanting help from overseas, even people like us! It remains a problem, however, how far at this stage in African history, we can stay in a situation which becomes very embarrassing to our African friends to explain away to their politically minded friends. These are not easy times. Many of our students shared in the Conference as stewards. They heard all that went on, and in the process of discussion they got hold of all that was being said, and at some points, more than was being said! They have come back this term very full indeed of critical and political emotional ideas. Life in college has never ever been quite like it is now, even during the Kabaka's exile. Everything we do or don't do, on the staff side, is suspect or downright wrong. It is not said despairingly on our part when we sum up the situation as "you just can't win".'

That sort of thing is a cross. Similarly highly charged emotional attitudes are to be found in many other parts of Africa and of the world. One leading missionary thinker has remarked about the missionary presence in Africa that for the next few years we will not be able to put a foot right, and whatever we do will be misunderstood and misrepresented. There is increasing evidence that he is correct.

I give two further illustrations of the kind of cross the Church makes for some of its missionaries. A conference-retreat was being held in a lovely city in South-east Asia. It was made up of Indians, Chinese and Westerners (including some from Australia and New Zealand). All the latter were missionaries from three different societies and working harmoniously. I was myself present at this conference and the bishop, himself a missionary, presided. At one point a young Indian clergyman exploded and poured out all his pent-up anger and resentment. He made a fierce attack on the missionaries for whom he had not one good word. He objected to any missionary taking any initiative in any matter. Some of the most promising projects in the church had in fact been started by missionaries and for this reason they were wrong. The missionaries just had to listen to this bitter outburst in silence and take it manfully. And not one of them answered back or showed any subsequent resentment. Yet they had to

hear their work misrepresented and their motives misunderstood. There was however something deeper behind this particular incident. The young man was an assistant minister at
a big town church whose congregation was racially mixed,
European, Indian, and Chinese. The vicar was a European
missionary who had gone home on furlough. When he went,
some European members, a quite typical cross-section of
church people such as you would find anywhere, had pledged
themselves to be loyal to the young Indian and to support him
whatever happened. They did this splendidly, but many Indians and Chinese ceased attending church within a short time.
Despite this love and backing from the European members,
instead of being pleased and grateful the Indian was more
anti-European than ever. This is life : this is the cross.

In many parts of South-east Asia there is not only resentment
against the presence of missionaries, needed as they are, but a
perpetual misunderstanding about the basic missionary motive
and their own personal reasons for being there. 'Missionaries
come here because they like our country more than their own.
Life is easier here and it is easier to make converts.' Variations
on this theme were offered on a number of occasions from
Chinese and Indians, usually by clergy, who can become
extraordinarily jealous, especially over matters of status. The
odd thing is that there is plenty of evidence that if a congregation were given a completely free choice as to what kind
of priest or minister they would have, a large number of inter-
racial congregations, and some of those predominantly Indian
or Chinese, would still ask for a European clergyman, largely
because of the missionaries' reputation for integrity and im-
partiality and devoted pastoral work. Over much of the world
it is in fact true that it is the indigenous clergy more often
than the laity that resent missionaries. It is a hard thing for
missionaries to have to bear these continual criticisms, some
of which are so patently untrue. No one who has lived in the
unvarying heat and humidity of Singapore could claim that it
is a pleasanter place to live in than Europe, neither can anyone
who has attempted evangelism in South-east Asia pretend
that it is easier than it is in the West.

I use these reminiscences with one purpose only in view. That purpose is not to apportion blame or to express criticism or indignation against any of those who were anti-missionary or anti-European. Many of them have good reasons for this from a *psychological* viewpoint. Missionaries have not always been guiltless. Some of the people who are opposed to missionaries and now bring their resentments into the open have themselves been bossed and pushed around by missionaries in the past or kept waiting on the verandah while the missionary finishes his meal. Or they remember—perhaps subconsciously—their fathers being treated like this a generation ago. I can recall hearing missionaries speak to Africans and Asians in a way that would be unthinkable to their fellow-Europeans. There is much for which missionaries must ask forgiveness. The best kind of missionary will be sensitive at this point and realize that he himself has constantly to receive forgiveness from those he serves. The sole purpose here is to write realistically about the kind of cross missionaries must bear today in these situations. And, like our Lord, we have to understand and to forgive, even though we ourselves may be misunderstood and unforgiven.

The hardest thing of all, of course, is that this cross is made by the Church—not by the non-Christian outsider. But the people of God, as portrayed in the Bible, have never been easy people. How shockingly they behaved to Moses! He had to suffer their grumbling and ingratitude for forty years. And what a time St Paul had with the Corinthians, as his correspondence with them shows! No church has ever been perfect. There is no model Christian community. And in every country, as most of us have discovered, not least in our own, some Christians can be much more difficult to get on with than good healthy pagans, who are often more reasonable and more attractive. But Christians are called and enabled to forbear and to forgive one another, as Christ forgives us. This can be costly for us, as it was for him. One of the ironies of the Christian mission is that its success always makes it harder for the missionaries. Before there is a church of any size and their work is chiefly among non-Christians it may be

unrewarding but it is generally uncomplicated and straight-
forward. It is infinitely more demanding to be a missionary
where there is an indigenous church with ideas of its own, as
in nearly all Africa and Asia and Latin America—but this is
as it should be, even if it does make a cross.

So today from an increasing number of places we hear the
cry 'Missionary, Go Home!' If this were the only cry and
represented unanimity, as it largely did in China around 1950,
it might well be the right thing to withdraw. But very often
this sentiment is voiced chiefly, if not solely, by clergy and
leaders, and behind it there still sounds another cry from
thousands of ordinary people: 'Come over and help us.' The
contradiction between the two creates a cross.

An Unresponsive People. Popularity is transitory and crowds
are fickle. Politicians and pop singers soon discover this from
the opinion polls. In the gospels we see Jesus alternating
between popularity and unpopularity. In Luke 4.28 one crowd
thrusts him out and tries to kill him; in Luke 4.42 another
crowd begs him not to leave them. At the beginning of John 6
a multitude follows him; at the end many of his disciples draw
back and leave him because he has said hard things. Jesus
always perceived the mixed motives in his followers: 'I know
that you have come looking for me because your hunger was
satisfied with the loaves you ate, not because you saw signs.
You must work, not for this perishable food, but for the food
that lasts, the food of eternal life' (John 6.26f). One Sunday a
huge crowd welcomes him into Jerusalem, shouting Hosanna;
the following Friday, another crowd—or was it largely the
same?—reject him, shouting Crucify. People are like this,
always, everywhere.

The missionary experience is not altogether dissimilar. So
long as missionaries can provide cheap teaching or healing or
free food, they are welcomed by most people. As soon as they
begin to challenge or to offer 'a new teaching' many of the
same people will regard them as a nuisance. As we saw in an
earlier chapter, today many of these works of service once
performed by missionaries and the Church have been rightly

taken over by the State. When they have nothing but the Gospel to offer missionaries are far less popular and often regarded as quite unnecessary. The motives that prompt response are still mixed. Thus, American powdered milk could be a great draw in India, cheap schooling a great asset in Africa, good hospitals and clinics a useful benefit in Muslim lands—but when, for various reasons, all this stops, if it has to, what then? The Church is left with nothing but the Gospel.

In some parts of the world the response has been negligible. A highly qualified and deeply devoted Lutheran missionary in Japan once told me that in ten years he had not seen a hundred baptisms. A Southern Baptist missionary of the USA in a different area gave a similar picture of unresponsiveness. In Aden where the Danish Church has for a long time had missionaries there are only one or perhaps two baptisms a year. Across the North-west Frontier of Pakistan, which borders Afghanistan, Russia and China, there is a chain of mission hospitals, working among the Pathans, attractive but wild and cruel tribes, fanatically Muslim, who live in those hills. Forty or fifty years ago there was a trickle of converts, but now there are none. Some missionaries with many years of service behind them have never yet seen a convert. They stay on, working, serving and loving an unresponsive people. This is their calling and their cross.

And even in areas where missionaries are welcomed by most people and enjoy their respect and trust, in a moment of crisis or tragedy this can suddenly turn to hatred. A missionary in Nigeria was driving along a road in a district where he was well known and his work had been valued over many years. There was a violent thunder-storm and in a nearby field he saw a boy struck by lightning. He stopped and went to the boy's help only to find he was dead. He put the boy in his car and took him to the village and to his family. The villagers immediately assumed that he had killed the boy himself; wild anger took hold of them and the missionary was only saved from being lynched to death by the intervention of the chief who believed his story. If it is not one kind of cross it is another.

The Friend that Failed. There are hints in the Gospels that Judas may have been more gifted than the rest of the Twelve. He was able to take responsibility and to look after the funds. He had political interests and access to the Jewish leaders. Dorothy Sayers suggested that he may have been something of an intellectual, shrewd and quick and perceptive. Jesus had chosen him, knowing his susceptibilities and the risk involved (John 6.70; 17.12). But greed and pride gained an increasing hold over Judas; he appears to have disagreed with the Lord's interpretation of Messiahship, and in a gesture of anger, impatience and despair he betrayed him to his enemies. Nevertheless, Judas was one of our Lord's intimate circle whom he had trusted. Judas rejected that last appeal at the supper table (John 13.26) even when he was singled out for favour, and he went into the night on his terrible errand. Part of the poignancy and pain of the Cross for Jesus must have been the treachery of Judas, his friend and disciple. No one who had such high regard for human relationships as Jesus could have been unhurt by such action. And the pain would have been at two levels. First, there was the realization that he had failed with Judas and lost him; second, there was the agony of remorse for Judas, which Jesus knew would follow but which he was powerless to prevent. The best can fail.

Once in Uganda some years ago I was visiting a famous leprosy settlement run by Christians, missionaries and others, Europeans and Africans. I found the European workers in profound distress. One of their number had committed suicide, and one of the finest and most promising young Africans, a deeply committed and mature Christian, trusted by everyone, had had to be dismissed from his post as head-master of the school because of a serious act of immorality. They were not judging him; they were mourning him.

I shall not easily forget a quiet conversation with a young woman missionary in South-east Asia, trying to hold back the tears, because the Chinese priest with whom she worked, a good man, kept treating her disgracefully. Far from receiving from him the help and encouragement she might have expected, she got little understanding or co-operation and was on the point of despair. These are the things that compose the modern missionary's cross.

But such anguish is not confined to younger churches. Here is a very moving description of a valiant piece of Christian social work among teenage drug addicts in East Harlem, New York. The chapter from which it is taken is entitled 'Crucifixion'.

'Out of sixteen kids who were in my Youth Group ten years ago, seven are addicts and one is dead through using drugs.' The pastor was not criticizing the youths. He was confessing his failure and expressing his grief; he was speaking indirectly of the cross his ministry entailed. For ten years, with the laymen in his church, he had stood alongside these youths, trying to sort out their problems, praying for them, finding them jobs, helping to make their lives whole. But slowly those lives had fallen apart and finally succumbed to the power of heroin, leaving young men who had once been gay and alert and optimistic now sitting listless in a corner of a candy store, their eyes glazed and heads nodding like helpless, mechanical dolls. And those who had worked, year in and year out, to help preserve those lives and make them strong knew what Paul meant when he said, 'We are partakers in the sufferings of Christ'; for it was an agonizing experience to watch one's friends descend into a living hell.[1]

A little later in the same chapter the writer tells of a happy Negro, who having been rescued from drugs finally relapsed and wrote:

Heroin is my shepherd
I shall always want
It maketh me to lie down in gutters
It leadeth me beside still madness
It destroyeth my soul
It leadeth me in the paths of Hell for its name's sake
Yea, though I walk through the Valley of the Shadow of Death
I will fear no evil
For heroin art with me

[1] Bruce Kenrick, *Come Out the Wilderness*, Collins 1963 and Fontana, 108.

My syringe and spike will comfort me
Thou puttest me to shame in the presence of mine enemies
Thou anointest my head with madness
My cup runneth over with sorrow
Surely hate and evil shall follow me all the days of my life
And I will dwell in the house of misery and disgrace for ever.

Those who had worked to save this man they so much loved felt something of the agony of Gethsemane and wanted to pray with Christ: 'Father, if it be possible, let this cup pass from me.' But it was not possible. The way for Christ had to be the way of the Cross, and that has to be the way of his servants too.[1]

In the New English Bible the heading given for II Corinthians 10-13 is *Trials of a Christian Missionary*. In those chapters Paul gives some account of his own cross. Those who engage in the same mission in the same world will know something of the same cross. And in certain moments the loneliness will be worse than the pain.

THE ACHIEVEMENT OF THE CROSS

Suffering and opposition can crush men or make them into saints. Jesus accepted the Cross and all that composed it, the shame and the pain, because he accepted his Father's will. He was able to look beyond the Cross into the future with complete faith and serenity. He could endure 'for the sake of the joy that lay ahead of him' (Heb. 12.2) and because of the glory he was to resume as he returned to his Father (John 17.1-5). It was his acceptance and bearing of the Cross, without resentment and without sin, which enabled his real mission to be accomplished and completed. So in the Johannine passion narrative the climax is the cry of victory and achievement: 'It is finished.' The Cross was redemptive not by virtue of any power in itself or in any form of suffering as such—there was nothing redemptive in the crosses or the sufferings of the two thieves—but because of what he did with it and made of it.

[1] Ibid., p. 218f.

He bent the Cross by his obedience to the Father's will. He made it into an instrument of salvation instead of destruction. He transformed its horror into a thing of wonderful beauty.

The passion of Jesus, beside being redemptive for the world, is also exemplary for the Church.

> Christ suffered on your behalf, and thereby left you an example; it is for you to follow in his steps. He committed no sin, he was convicted of no falsehood; when he was abused he did not retort with abuse, when he suffered he uttered no threats, but committed his cause to the One who judges justly (I Peter 2.21-3).

The Church is called to the imitation of Christ at the level of his mission and passion as well as his life and character. And for those who move towards this, on the other side of pain, sorrow, disappointment, vicarious suffering, there is some spiritual achievement on behalf of others, there is joy ahead, and beyond every cross there is a resurrection experience. There can be redemptive value in all our setbacks and failures, if we accept them as a cross and bear them creatively as Jesus bore his. It may be only as some people see the cross being borne silently in the life of some contemporary Christian that they will grasp something of the meaning of the great Cross, when God himself was the bearer, and perceive the agony of the Strong.

There is always a cross where holiness meets with sin. The uniqueness of Christ's Cross is that there in one man's body and will, the full and perfect holiness of God met with the sin of all the world. The reality of our crosses is that our very partial holiness, namely the fact that we belong to Jesus Christ and are dedicated to him, meets with resentment and resistance inevitably in that segment of the world where we try to witness and serve. If we meet this resistance with love a cross will form. No one has expounded this concept more powerfully than P. T. Forsyth who, writing of Christ, said:

> His holiness takes its own consequences in an evil world. . . . There is no way but the Cross of committing a holy love to

such a world as this. The Gospel of a holy God is not soon popular. The holier your love is the more you will suffer and be rejected with it. God almighty knew, for himself even, no way but the Cross to the hearts and wills of evil men.[1]

In all mission the means is a cross, the end a resurrection. We know something of the meaning of the cross; we know little of the meaning of the end or the resurrection. But both are on their way, and every writer in the Bible expects them to be glorious.

[1] P. T. Forsyth, *Revelation Old and New*, Independent Press 1962, 11, 14.

INDEX

Easier to reject to than reject here. 91.